"We travel together, passengers on a little spaceship, dependent on its vulnerable reserves of air and soil; all committed for our safety to its security and peace; preserved from annihilation only by the care, the work, and, I will say, the love we give our fragile craft. We cannot maintain it half fortunate, half miserable, half confident, half despairing, half slave to the ancient enemies of man, half free in a liberation of resources undreamed of until this day. No craft, no crew can travel safely with such vast contradictions. On their resolution depends the survival of us all."   **Adlai Stevenson**

"One world—or none."   **Wendell L. Willkie**

HOW TO BE
A SURVIVOR

PAUL R. EHRLICH

Dr. Paul R. Ehrlich, Professor of Biology and Director of Graduate Studies at Stanford University, is a population biologist and ecologist whose studies convinced him some years ago that "if *Homo Sapiens* is to continue as the dominant species of life on Earth, modern man must come soon to a better understanding of the Earth and of what he has been doing to it." In his subsequent efforts to inform and convince others about the elements and dimensions of the overpopulation crisis, Professor Ehrlich has become probably the nation's most outspoken expert on the subject. He graduated from the University of Pennsylvania and received M.A. and Ph.D. degrees from the University of Kansas; he has lectured on more than 150 college campuses, has testified before congressional groups, and has written many scientific and popular articles and several books, including the best-selling paperback *The Population Bomb* (1971).

RICHARD L. HARRIMAN

Mr. Richard L. Harriman is a graduate student in Political Science at Stanford University. Through his close association with Dr. Ehrlich, Mr. Harriman has worked extensively with the subject of the population crisis and its relationship with environmental deterioration. His interests are in New Politics, the political implications of the ecological movement and new life styles.

HOW TO BE
A SURVIVOR

Dr. Paul R. Ehrlich
and
Richard L. Harriman

BALLANTINE BOOKS, LTD.
An Intertext Publisher
LONDON • NEW YORK

First U.S. Printing: January, 1971
First U.K. Printing: October, 1971

Printed in Canada.

Ballantine Books, Ltd.
8 King Street
London, WC2E 8HS

Distributor: Pan Books, Ltd.

To
Loy Bilderback
Douglas Daetz
Thomas Harriman, Jr.
John Hessel
John Holdren
Richard Holm
John Montgomery
John Thomas

Contents

Appendices 141

Authors' Note

Scientists in our society are often criticized for being too narrow, but when they step outside the narrow field of their training they are invariably told they should stick to their specialty We prefer to risk the latter criticism. In many areas of this book, we have gone beyond the boundaries of our formal training to try to seek solutions to human problems. We see no other course than for scientists in all fields to do the same—even at the risk of being wrong.

Paul R. Ehrlich
Richard L. Harriman

HOW TO BE
A SURVIVOR

I

Spaceship in Trouble

IN APRIL 1970, an explosion occurred on board the spaceship Apollo 13, seriously affecting its life-support systems and threatening the lives of its three crewmen. Fortunately, careful planning for emergencies had been carried out in advance by NASA technicians, and rapid decisions about emergency action were possible. Such decisions were made, the astronauts performed with courage and ingenuity and were able to survive the mission.

That very same April a much larger spaceship was also in deep trouble. Its life-support systems were malfunctioning, it was running out of vital supplies, and half of its overcrowded passengers were hungry. But on this spaceship there had been no emergency planning; indeed, there was not even any crew. Most of the first-class passengers were under the impression that the ship existed only for their benefit, and spent their time squabbling with each other and maneuvering to insure themselves the lion's share of the dwindling stores. The tourist and steerage passengers lived and died mostly in misery, unable to get their fair share and unaware that even a fair share was by then inadequate. That spaceship was, and is, the Spaceship Earth.

By April 1970, a scattering of the passengers had perceived the danger to their vessel. Over the last few hundred years of the Ship's long voyage there had been occasional warnings from individuals concerned with the functioning of the life-support systems, but until the 1960's their words went unheeded. Then, in the last few years of that decade, signs of malfunctioning were sufficiently obvious and frequent to attract wide attention. On April 22, 1970—for the first time in history—a substantial number of the passengers of Spaceship Earth paused to consider the state of their vehicle. That day was, hopefully, the first step in organizing the passengers into a crew for the endangered Ship, and in taking the actions necessary for survival.

This book is designed to be a step toward the development of a survival manual for Spaceship Earth. It contains a brief description of the state of the Ship in mid-1970, and then gives suggestions for emergency procedures and long-term actions which we feel are essential for the successful continuation of our voyage. In some cases we will be very specific about solutions. In others, we will merely indicate the direction in which we feel solutions might lie. Finally, we are including a set of actions which may be taken immediately by individuals who have an interest in their own survival and quality of life, and that of their children and subsequent generations.

The State of the Ship: Today and Tomorrow[1]

Passengers. Approximately 3.6 billion human beings are aboard Spaceship Earth. Almost one half of these are "hungry"—that is, they are undernourished or malnourished. Between 10 and 20 million passengers, a

---

[1] Unless otherwise cited, details and supporting references for statements made in this book may be found in P. R. Ehrlich and A. H. Ehrlich, *Population, Resources, Environment: Issues in Human Ecology* (San Francisco: W. H. Freeman and Company, 1970.)

great many of them children, now starve to death annually. The most serious nutritional problem is malnourishment which usually results from a lack of high quality protein in the diet. Protein malnourishment, if it does not result in death, all too often produces mental retardation. Without an adequate supply of protein, the body is unable to manufacture enough brain tissue.

The quarters for most of the passengers are substandard or worse. As Professor Georg Borgstrom of Michigan State University recently put it: ". . . there are not many oases left in a vast, almost world-wide network of slums." [2] The scale of needed slum clearance is difficult to comprehend. For instance, if it were possible to construct 10,000 houses per day in Latin America for the next decade, about 100 million people there would still be ill-housed at the end of that period.

But crowded, hungry, and miserable as much of mankind is today, tomorrow seems destined to be much worse. The passenger list of our spaceship is growing by roughly *70 million persons annually*. Every three years, 210 million people—a population slightly larger than that of the United States—are added to the planet. The growth rate is so rapid and the numbers so large that it is difficult for us to grasp their meaning. Perhaps the most stunning way of driving home the rate of world population growth is to compare it with the horrifying statistics of war. In all the wars the United States has fought—the Revolution, the War of 1812, the Mexican War, the Civil War, the Spanish-American War, World Wars I and II, Korea, Vietnam, Laos and Cambodia—the United States has had some 600,000 men killed in battle. The size of the world population now increases by 600,000 people every three and a half days.

As population increases and as people are crowded more and more into urban areas, the probabilities of plague and conflict also grow. And each individual's chances for leading a fulfilling, happy life shrink.

---

[2] Georg Borgstrom, *Too Many: The Biological Limitations of Our Earth* (New York: Macmillan, 1970), p. xi.

Supplies. Economist Abba Lerner of the University of California summarized the resource situation of Spaceship Earth in a single sentence. "If you want to improve the standard of living of mankind, you basically have two choices: make the Earth larger or make the population smaller." [3] No matter how you slice it, the resources of the planet are finite, and many of them are non-renewable. Each giant molecule of petroleum is lost forever when we tear it asunder by burning to release the energy of sunlight stored in it millions of years ago. Concentrations of mineral wealth are being dispersed beyond recall, senselessly scattered far and wide to where we cannot afford the energy to reconcentrate them.[4] Precious stores of fresh ground water, accumulated over millennia, are being drained much more rapidly than natural processes can replenish them.

This profligate use of resources results in part from desperate attempts to provide bare subsistence for most of mankind. But it also derives from the exploitative economic systems of the overdeveloped nations, which persist in the pursuit of an "affluence" based on almost limitless wastage. Since the non-renewable resources consumed by these wastrels are resources which will not be available to their descendants, this behavior has been accurately described as grand larceny against the future. We are doing something that few businessmen would consider rational in conducting their own businesses. We are rapidly using up our capital in full knowledge that it will be impossible to get any more.

Life-Support Systems. If too many people in relation to

[3] Debate January 14, 1970 at the University of California, Berkeley, sponsored by the Northern California Committee for Environmental Information.

[4] Energy use always pollutes. Vast amounts of energy are used to mine concentrated ores. The amounts that would be necessary to attempt, say, to reclaim rusted iron scattered thinly over the Earth's surface by man would be incalculably higher. Even if the energy were available (it is not), the impact of its use on the ecology of the planet would be disastrous.

food and other resources were our only problem, Professor Lerner's alternatives would summarize the possible solutions. We could get out of our troubles either by increasing the amount of resources ("making the earth larger") or by reducing population size. Indeed, many people see the world situation in just these simple terms. But things are not that simple. Population growth itself greatly increases environmental deterioration.[5] Rapidly accelerating environmental deterioration adds enormous complexity and difficulty to the existing population-resource imbalance.

Most laymen tend to view environmental deterioration (which they think of as "pollution") as a problem combining esthetic decay and direct health hazards. It is quite true, of course, that we are turning the world into a vast slum and junkyard, and that pollutants are reducing our life expectancy. DDT alone may already have substantially reduced the statistical life expectancy of all of us, especially of children born since 1948.

More important than these obvious hazards though, are the subtle, indirect threats of environmental deterioration. These are threats to the integrity of the life-support systems of our spaceship—the ecological systems (ecosystems) of our planet. We must always remember two facts.

First, we are all completely dependent on the life-support systems of our planet for every bit of our food, for the oxygen in our atmosphere, for the purity of that atmosphere, and for the disposal of our wastes. Green plants supply our oxygen and our food. All animals eat either plants or other animals, which in turn eat plants or eat animals that eat animals, which in turn eat plants, and so forth. (In spite of what some Americans seem to think, food does not materialize miraculously overnight in supermarkets.) Without green plants we would all quickly starve to death. Even if we could live without food, we would eventually suffocate in the

---

[5] The relationship between population growth and environmental deterioration is detailed in Appendix II.

absence of green plants. We would slowly use up the store of oxygen which plants have created in the atmosphere over millions of years, and then there would be no more. In addition to green plants, a variety of microorganisms (tiny bacteria, protozoa, and fungi) work quietly in soil and water recycling the materials necessary for life, and in the process they too maintain the quality of the atmosphere.

The second important fact to remember is that the stability of ecological systems depends in large part on their complexity. Every time a population or species is driven into extinction, every time prairie is cleared and planted with a single crop, every time an area is paved, the complexity of the Earth's ecosystem is reduced, and the danger of large scale malfunctions of the life-support systems of the planet is increased. Suspicious signs of such malfunctioning are already apparent in our lakes, rivers, and even in the oceans.

Suppose our lives depended on the smooth functioning of a complex computer. We are aware of the general principles of the computer's design. For instance we know that it often has more than one transistor where one would suffice, providing the safety of redundancy. Now, suppose we see to our horror that people and machines are beginning to pull transistors from the computer at random. We cannot predict accurately when the computer will stop functioning, because we don't know exactly how "fail-safe" the various back-up systems make it. But we can be sure that if enough transistors are removed, the computer will stop or malfunction and we will die.

Similarly, ecologists cannot predict exactly when or how the world ecosystem—the life-support system of our spaceship—will break down. However, we can guarantee that, if our present course is continued, sooner or later *it will break down.* Preliminary signs make "sooner" seem more likely than "later."

In addition to ecosystem simplification, other subtle kinds of environmental deterioration also present grave threats. For example, air pollution is now changing the climate of the Earth. As more and more marginal land is farmed, large quantities of dust are picked up by the wind and carried long distances in the atmosphere, creating such meteorological phenomena as the Harmattan haze of Africa and a dust "blanket" over much of southern Asia. The overdeveloped countries pour huge amounts of poisonous gases and solid particles into the atmosphere, both from industry and from automobiles. As a result, the murkiness of the atmosphere over the central Pacific Ocean—far from major sources of contamination—has increased 30 per cent in the last decade. One consequence of this massive injection of particles into the atmosphere has been a cooling trend resulting from the decreased ability of sunlight to penetrate the atmosphere. An alternate trend is known as the "greenhouse" effect. Either could undoubtedly lead to weather changes which, in turn, would hurt world agriculture. Such changes could seriously damage American agriculture as early as the decade of the 70's. Since we have only about one year's reserve supply of food in the United States, famine could come to this nation, and it could come relatively soon. The blight in the corn belt in 1970, associated with too moist weather, may be a foretaste of things to come.

Perhaps the most threatening change in our environment is directly related to increased population size and the resulting food scarcity. The larger and denser our population becomes, the greater is the probability of a worldwide plague. Remember that there are more hunger-weakened people in the world today than there were people in 1875. This large, weak population is a perfect target for disease-causing organisms—especially for a lethal virus. A lethal epidemic might result from a mutation of a virus already present in the human population, such as the flu. The chance of such a mutation's occurring goes up as the number of people (and thus the number of human viruses) increases.

Alternatively, we might be struck down by a plague

of animal origin. We may have come close in 1967. In that year a virus never before recorded in human beings transferred from vervet monkeys to laboratory workers in Marburg, Germany, and Yugoslavia. The "Marburgvirus" as it became known was both extremely contagious and lethal. About thirty people were infected before the disease was contained, and seven died. Seven died even though they had excellent medical care, were well-fed, and were neither very young nor very old. What might have been the mortality had this virus escaped into the world population? Since the answer would depend upon the exact mode of transmission and whether or not the virulence of the virus changed as it passed through the large population, we do not know. But, considering that most people in the world do not have medical care, that about half are poorly fed, and that 37 per cent are under 15 years of age (children are more susceptible to disease), the possibility of a majority of mankind being killed clearly existed. The monkeys carrying the virus were in the London airport two weeks before the incident at Marburg. If the transfer of the virus to man had occurred at the airport, the disease might have spread over most of the world before the peril was recognized.

Sad to say, we don't have to depend on an event involving natural viruses or bacteria for a worldwide pestilence. In many countries unthinking scientists are busily at work in biological warfare laboratories *constructing* lethal organisms. Since there is no such thing as an "escape-proof" virus laboratory, these activities have an enormous potential for disaster, even if the weapons are never deliberately used. Already, one virus disease—Venezuelan Equine Encephalitis—may have escaped from U. S. biological warfare laboratories. It has been reported to be established among wild animals in Utah.[6]

Finally, we must point out that increasing population size also means an increasing probability of thermo-

---

[6] UP story, May 9, 1969, *San Francisco Chronicle*.

nuclear war. The resources of the planet are finite, and as the population grows each person's "share" of those resources decreases. This is one source of what political scientist Robert C. North calls "lateral pressure"—expansionism by nations, which often leads to war. One recent war almost entirely due to population pressures was that between El Salvador and Honduras in 1969. El Salvador had a population density of 782 people per square mile of arable land. Honduras, although overpopulated, was in relatively better shape with only 155 persons per square mile of arable land. Population pressure at home had forced almost ⅓ million Salvadorans to move to Honduras seeking jobs, and the ambitious immigrants were unpopular in Honduras. The Hondurans were accused by El Salvador of mistreating the immigrants, and the situation escalated into a bloody conflict. The war was finally stopped by the Organization of American States (OAS), which officially recognized population pressure as its major cause.

Population-resource problems are clearly involved in areas of world conflict today, especially in the Middle East where the policies of major powers always include consideration of the rich oil resources of the region. The same applies to Southeast Asia with its large reserves of tin and rubber and its enormous potential for petroleum development. As the population grows and resource consumption increases, greater friction will be generated. This will be exacerbated by international conflicts over two resources rarely considered: fresh water and clean air. Preventing these conflicts from snowballing into a thermonuclear götterdämmerung will take a combination of enormous diplomatic skill and good luck.

Should we lack the skill, the luck, or both, the resulting war will be a disaster unprecedented in the history of mankind. The soldiers, politicians, businessmen, and "scientists" who have tried to project the results of such a war have largely ignored the ecological and psychological problems it would cause. At least part of the military-industrial complex is anticipating a thermonuclear war, discussing its "advantages" and planning to survive and rebuild a wonderful anti-communist system afterwards. They point out that Hiroshima is completely recovered and prosperous today, and that tuberculosis (now largely confined to central cities) would disappear. But they worry about *too many* survivors causing a labor-capital imbalance! They have built underground retreats and data-storage facilities. One bank, Manufacturers Hanover Trust, has detailed plans for collecting outstanding debts after the attack. *They are serious.* Here is a sample[7] of their own words:

"Our studies indicate that we would have the capability, and, given the will, we can emerge from such a holocaust to maintain a dominant position in the world and sustain the Western values we cherish."
> —Lloyd B. Addington,
> Office of the Chief of Engineers,
> U. S. Army

"I would like to emphasize that our emergency planning is predicated on the idea that it is possible for our nation to survive, recover, and win, and that our way of life, including free enterprise, the oil industry, and Socony Mobil Oil Company, can survive, recover, and win with it."
> —Maxwell S. McKnight, security adviser of
> Socony Mobil Oil Company.

Even if biological, radiological, and chemical warfare were not used, the detonation of a large number of "clean" H-bombs could shatter the ecological balance of the plant. Large areas would be burned, vast amounts of debris would be swept into the atmosphere, and huge amounts of silt mixed with chemical poisons from de-

[7] A more detailed discussion of the material in this and in the preceding paragraph may be found in John H. Rothchild's "Civil Defense: The Case for Nuclear War" (*Washington Monthly,* October 1970), pp. 34-46 from which these quotes were extracted.

stroyed storage tanks would pour into the sea. The people surviving the blast and radiation would face an extremely hostile environment. If we can judge from relatively minor past disasters, such as the black plague and the Irish potato famine, the survivors would also be psychologically devastated.

If it were not possible to keep civilization going, it would soon be impossible to start it up again. We are beyond the point where man might start over again, after a lapse of hundreds or thousands of years, to rebuild a technological society. The high grade resources necessary for such rebuilding are no longer available—rich, surface copper deposits are long since dispersed; oil no longer bubbles to the surface. We need technology to get at the raw materials necessary to maintain technology. Once the cycle is broken, it cannot be restarted.

So, it is clear that Spaceship Earth is in deep trouble. But the situation is not hopeless—indeed we can probably survive the current crisis and set mankind on the path to a long and pleasant space voyage. We can, that is, *if* we dramatically change the ways in which we treat both our fellow passengers and our vessel. And that is what this book is all about.

II

Principles of Spaceship Operation

An Idealized World

SUPPOSE YOU WERE to walk into the office of an aerospace engineer and ask him to design a jet transport or spaceship for you. One of the first things he would want to know is the number of people the craft would be expected to carry. If you answered that question with "Oh, design it for a constantly growing number of passengers," the engineer would, of course, decide that you are a hopeless nut and throw you out. No one in his right mind would try to design a passenger vehicle without knowing at least approximately how many passengers it was to carry. Nevertheless, right now a great many scientists and technologists are busily trying to manipulate the design of Spaceship Earth so that it can accommodate a constantly growing number of people, and all too many of these scientists seem unaware of the fundamental insanity of the process.

Perhaps you think that the life-support systems of our spaceship should be designed to provide the "greatest good for the greatest number." This cannot be done because it involves a double maximization, which is mathematically impossible. What must be done is to determine how much "good" should be available for each person. Then, just how many people can enjoy that much "good"

12

on a permanent basis can be determined, at least in theory. That number of people would then be one "optimum" population size for our finite planet.

Consider for a moment what form the amount of "good" that each person could enjoy might take. Some considerations seem rather elementary. Each human being should have available:

1. a diet adequate both in calories and in nutritional balance

2. adequate housing and clothing appropriate to the climate in which he or she lives

3. an environment in which the direct and indirect dangers of pollution are minimized

4. medical care sufficient to minimize the chances of disability or premature death from disease.

Although these requisites are somewhat hedged by qualifying terms such as "adequate" and "minimized," the determination of what resources are necessary to provide them is certainly possible. Problems arise, however, when we consider less concrete kinds of "good," those associated with the psychological rather than the physical state of the individual. People differ very widely in culturally (and possibly genetically) determined requirements for leading a fulfilling existence. This diversity is not just a difficult fact of life, it is a treasure which our species must preserve. Not only does it, in the eyes of many, add interest to human existence, it is also a reservoir of adaptability to draw on when cultural change is required for survival. It would be a serious error, for instance, to allow the extinction of the Australian aboriginal culture. After all, perhaps hidden among the aborigines' complex perceptions of kinship is a cultural secret that could be used by a world government to help persuade nations to settle their differences ritually rather than through violence. One has only to explore the work of anthropologists such as Margaret

Mead to appreciate the immense understanding of themselves that Westerners have derived from the study of non-Western cultures. We might never have gained such understanding, had all of human culture been homogenized in 1800.

We must preserve and plan for cultural diversity, then. There must be a place on our spaceship for Australian Aborigines and Eskimos, Taoists and Christians. The "good" in our world must allow for both hermits and big-city swingers. Thus the population must be small enough to permit solitude for the former and large enough to produce crowds for the latter.

Evil must be controlled in our design of an optimum system as surely as "good" must be included. War is insanity on a spaceship—it must be outlawed. So must racism and all other attitudes that result in the deprecation of diversity. Exploitation of one group of passengers by another must be made impossible. Each individual human being must have a maximum of freedom, limited only by the boundaries where his freedoms may encroach on others.

In short, we should design for an earthly paradise. We may never achieve it, but to design for any other goal would be pointless.

The Conversion Process

Whether or not we will eventually achieve even an approximation of paradise, dramatic changes in the living arrangements on Spaceship Earth must commence immediately. The directions in which we must move are clear; the conversion process is, in outline, simple.

1. Population control must be achieved in both overdeveloped countries (ODCs) and underdeveloped countries (UDCs).
2. The ODCs must be de-developed.
3. The UDCs must be semi-developed.

4. The procedures must be set up for monitoring and regulating the world system in a continuous effort to maintain an optimum population-resource-environment situation.

Obviously, enormous complexity and endless difficulty is concealed in that brief outline. There are many questions implicit in it. Can we, for instance, persuade the United States to move along the road to population control? What would be the most efficient way of achieving such control? Can the life styles of Americans be changed sufficiently to permit the United States to de-develop—that is, to move from an enormously wasteful and ecologically dangerous "cowboy economy" to a safe, resource-conserving "spaceman economy?" If we start toward population control and de-development can the other ODCs be persuaded to join us? Would they co-operate with us to extend a massive helping hand to the UDCs? Would any UDCs accept our aid in the areas of population control and semi-development?

The main initiative must, for the moment, rest with ODCs, and especially with the U.S.A. The ODCs and UDCs have fundamentally different world views. In the ODCs, people are concerned with maintaining or increasing affluence, and keeping the international system working. To a much more limited extent, they are concerned about the quality of the world environment and the "plight" of the UDCs. Their concern for the UDCs virtually always has contained an element of self-interest: they don't want their lovely boat rocked. This concern is usually also loaded with cultural chauvinism: they would like the UDCs to develop along the same marvelous lines as today's ODCs.

Those who lead the UDCs, on the other hand, naturally take a more parochial view. They have almost all been educated in ODCs themselves, or by people who were trained in ODCs. They have "bought" most of the value systems of Western culture hook, line, and sinker. But they are have-nots, eager for a share of the action.

Like their counterparts in the ODCs, they do not question the fundamental assumptions underlying their attitudes and values. Industrialization is an absolute good. Material affluence is an absolute good. Property is more important than people. The list goes on and on.

Those in power in the UDCs, while scorning the exploitative behavior of the ODCs, make it perfectly clear that they would move heaven and earth for a chance to behave in the same way. Unhappily, but understandably, they are much less likely to question the assumptions of the Western system than are their counterparts in the ODCs. In addition, they have the very real whipping boys of past colonialism and present economic exploitation to blame for their troubles. Therefore, they are less inclined to face realistically the internal components of their national problems. They are encouraged to hold an optimistic view of the problem of development by the approach of Western scientists who are involved in development programs. These scientists characteristically avoid mention of embarrassing internal problems in the UDCs. As Gunnar Myrdal[1] put it, "The tendency to think and act in a diplomatic manner when dealing with the problems of the underdeveloped countries has, in the new era of independence, become a new version of the 'white man's burden.' If the intellectuals in underdeveloped countries understood how much this approach to their problems is tantamount to condescension, they would feel offended."[2] Ironically then, hope for reform of the present inequitable and exploitative

---

[1] Gunnar Myrdal, *The Challenge of World Poverty* (New York: Pantheon, 1970), p. 8.

[2] There is a moral corollary to what Myrdal notes here. One of the greatest bloodlettings of the 1960's was in the Sudan. Arabicized, neutralist-left-leaning Sudanese simply decided to eliminate the animistic tribal Sudanese of the south. This hardly made a ripple in the American press, and was not mentioned in the United Nations. The reason is subtly racist. White moral superiority is assumed, and when it is flagrantly breached as at My Lai or by Mike Hoar's mercenaries in the Congo, we are horrified. But similar acts by non-Westerners are seen, at least

world system rests primarily with those most responsible for creating it. Most citizens of ODCs have their share of the action, and at least some of them can turn their thoughts to the value of that share—at what expense to themselves and others it was obtained, and what future difficulties, for themselves and others, maintaining it will entail. Poor citizens of the ODCs, as well as the poor nations of the world, will understandably remain engrossed in their own primary problem: eliminating poverty. It will be up to the ODCs both to extend massive aid toward that goal, *and to cooperate with the UDCs in defining new standards of non-poverty.*

The United States, as the richest and most powerful of the ODCs, is in the best position to assume leadership in the reorganization of Spaceship Earth. But leadership in this case, means leadership by example. We must come to recognize our large role in the exploitation of the resources of the Earth; we must recognize our massive contributions to the deterioration of the life-support systems of the Earth; and we must recognize the seriousness of our own population growth, both for ourselves and for the planet as a whole. Having recognized these things, we must begin a massive effort to correct them, and to persuade other ODCs to take similar steps. Once the ODCs are moving in the right direction, the extremely serious task of helping the UDCs can be approached. This task is difficult because of the physical, biological, and cultural constraints under which it must be accomplished. But it is made even more difficult by the well-deserved suspicion with which ODC motives are viewed in UDCs. People of the UDCs are not anxious for

---

unconsciously, as "the natural acts of lesser beings." Nasser used phosgene (a war gas) in Yemen where he was involved in pure, nineteenth-century, imperialistic expansion with the aim of grabbing Arabian oil. Another blatant example was the Hausa massacre of the Ibo, which led to the Biafran affair. A similar form of racism is found within the United States in the tendency of law enforcement agencies to prosecute whites who commit crimes against whites more vigorously than they do blacks who commit crimes against blacks.

"solutions" imposed by the powerful ODCs. Ways must be found for ODC economic assistance to flow through neutral channels to the UDCs, and to see that the pattern of those channels is, at least in part, determined by the UDCs themselves.

In the next four chapters, we will artificially separate the problem into four parts—population control, de-development of ODCs, semi-development of UDCs, and national-international controls—in order to suggest possible directions for action.

III

The Size of the Crew

ONCE OPTIMUM POPULATION size "targets" have been established for the entire world and for each country and area, the serious problems of how these targets are to be reached must be faced. But the first task, the establishment of targets, seems at the moment to be even more formidable. If a consensus on optimum size can be achieved, it will automatically mean that people have accepted the notion of population control. The change from an essentially laissez-faire attitude toward population growth to recognition of the need for national manipulation by society of population size is the critical first step toward control.

It is our contention that the long-term survival of our civilization, and perhaps even of our species, depends on everyone moving from the status of passenger to that of crewman. A passenger is just along for the ride and is usually unconcerned with the state of the ship. A crew member, on the other hand, spends at least part of each day involved in seeing that the voyage continues smoothly. Similarly, each human being must now spend at least part of his time in activities relevant to the voyage of the Spaceship Earth and the well-being of the rest of the crew. The place for each of us to begin our involvement is in determining the size of the crew, for no other single factor is more basic to the prolonged, proper functioning of the Ship. The problem of population control must be solved if we are to avoid disaster.

Population Control in the U.S.A.

On June 7, 1970 a hesitant but significant step was taken toward the control of the American population—though a step unnoted by most Americans. On that date the *First National Congress on Optimum Population and Environment* convened in Chicago. The purpose of the Congress was to open a dialogue which, it was hoped, would eventually lead to a consensus about the kind of environment in which Americans wanted to live and the size of population which could be supported while preserving that environment. The Congress was attended by scientists and laymen from most geographical areas and most walks of life.

As one might have predicted, the Congress did not run smoothly. It was clear that even many of the scientists were unfamiliar with the dimensions of the problem; demographers made ignorant statements about ecology, and biologists showed a lack of appreciation for the sociological facts of life. Many delegates still were laboring under the misapprehension that overpopulation was simply a matter of too many people per unit area, and were unaware of the resource-environment dimensions of the problem. Furthermore, minority groups felt, with some justification, that not enough effort had been made by the organizers of the Congress to include them among the leadership and to consider their special problems. In spite of the on-the-spot attempts to correct the situation, the black caucus walked out, leaving the door open, however, for future participation.

Still, the Congress was a step forward. Some members of the white majority learned that their concern for the purity of trout streams was not shared by blacks, who wanted to talk about features of ghetto environments, such as the population explosion of rats and roaches.

Some members of the black minority learned that many whites share their concern that population control should not be, in any sense, genocidal. There was a rather thorough exchange of information among the diverse people concerned with population-environment problems, and a general agreement that the dialogue should be continued with further Congresses.

Hopefully, these Congresses will provide some basis for deciding how far below the present level of 205 million people the population of the United States should be. Final decisions on that figure will, of course, depend in part on planetary planning. Strict limits will have to be placed on the resource consumption and pollution output of all nations, and planning by the United States will have to take such factors into account. It is certain that the eventual optimum for the United States will be well below the present size, and yet the demographic situation makes it abundantly clear that only enormous effort (or some disaster) can prevent our population from skyrocketing to 300 million or more by the early part of the next century.

What form should such an effort take? Most Americans seem to agree that governmental interference in the lives of individual citizens is already too great. Therefore, although governmental action is needed, it certainly should be taken in a manner which starts by offering maximum incentives with a minimum of coercion, and proceeds to more coercive measures only if more agreeable programs fail. Above all, no effort should be made to single out the poor, people on welfare, or nonwhites as special targets for population control; the middle class (made up mostly of whites) and the wealthy (almost entirely white) should be the primary targets. There are several reasons for this. First, the vast majority of American babies are born into white, middle-class families. Second, it is among the middle class and the wealthy that population growth presents the most serious problems. Although the growth *rate* in this segment of our population is slightly lower than that among the poor and the nonwhites, that tells only part of the story.

It is the affluent groups whose patterns of consumption are wasting the resources of our planet and destroying its environment. They buy the endless rounds of new cars, TV sets, appliances, and powered gadgets. They produce the bulk of our demand for power, both by direct use and by creating the power needs of industry (it takes power to *build* cars and appliances as well as to run them). Smog-producing coal-fired plants and potentially deadly nuclear power plants are not being built helter-skelter to meet the power demands of ghettos! We are not eating up the world's supplies of petroleum so that the poor can ricochet around the world in jet aircraft. We do not loot the underdeveloped world of its protein to feed farm animals so that people living in poverty can enjoy steaks, pork chops, and chicken.

Indeed our poor citizens and our nonwhite citizens are all too often the victims of the pollution related to affluence. Chicanos (Mexican-Americans) sicken and die in the agricultural areas of California because of the misuse of pesticides. Nonwhites seem to have higher loads of DDT in their bodies than whites, possibly because they are forced to eat a lower quality, fattier diet. The middle class and the wealthy normally can afford to move out of the central-city environmental disaster areas. They can live upwind of heavy industry or in the suburbs beyond the heavy smog belt, avoiding the deadly effluent which may increase the chances of contracting such diseases as emphysema, heart disease, lung cancer and other cancers.

It is, therefore, imperative that runaway population growth be curbed among the most dangerous elements of our society—those who are wasting our spaceship's limited stock of supplies and destroying its fragile life-support systems. Of course, as we curb their population growth we must also curb their destructive behavior, for even a limited population that behaves like today's affluent Americans would eventually destroy the planet.

There is, of course, a bonus to focusing our population control efforts on the rich and the middle class. We can allay the fears of the poor and nonwhite. They are understandably suspicious of the motives of affluent whites preaching population control. "Whose population is to be controlled?" they ask. And why shouldn't they? Too many ignorant and bigoted people would like to lay the blame for our country's woes on "those women on welfare" or "black women with large families." A prominent engineer, with little knowledge of population genetics, psychology, or anthropology, recently waged a campaign implying that blacks are genetically inferior in intelligence to whites. His lightly veiled message comes through loud and clear to the Ku Klux Klan mentality. The elements in our society who might try to solve our population problem by genocidally eliminating some of our priceless genetic diversity seem very close to the surface these days.

The best way to avoid any hint of genocide is to control the population of the dominant group. If this means an increase in the proportion of dark-skinned people in our society, so what? [1] If blacks and whites cannot learn to enjoy their differences instead of using them as a basis for hatred, there will not be a world worth living in. If they do learn to live together with mutual cultural enrichment, then the exact mix of colors will be of little consequence.

Of course, there is not a shred of evidence that members of other minority groups or "races" are in any way biologically "inferior" to whites or even to white Anglo-Saxon Protestants. Indeed, the classification of peoples into "races" is purely an arbitrary and artificial one. While any two samples of humanity from different places will differ in a wide array of attributes—many of them genetically determined—men do not fall into a neat set of races. It is no more logical to divide up mankind on the basis of skin color than it is to divide it on the basis

---

[1] In the early years of the United States, blacks comprised about twenty-five percent of the population.

of blood groups, and the divisions based on one set of characteristics do not coincide with those based on the other. Present day "races" are largely sociological, not biological, phenomena. Slightly different growth rates among racial groups should be viewed with equanimity.

Remember also that birth rates seem generally tied to economic and social status. Thus, when our country finally gets around to practicing what it preaches and gives all of its citizens equal access to affluence, one can expect population growth rates among different groups to converge. At the moment, although birth rates among poor blacks are somewhat higher than among poor whites, affluent blacks tend to have fewer children than affluent whites. Therefore those who are disturbed at the thought of a slightly higher proportion of blacks in our population have an excellent strategy open to them to lower the black birthrate: they should simply bend every effort to see to it that all blacks become affluent!

Before moving on to the steps that the U.S. government should be taking towards population control, consider for a moment a related area—family planning. The basic premise of family planning is that no woman should bear more children (or fewer children) than she wants. Children should be planned, both as to number and spacing. While people today may plan to have too many children (from the point of view of society), few would argue that family planning is not a social good. In the United States, although avoidance of all unwanted births would reduce our population growth rate, it would not halt population growth entirely.[2] Women should above all be able to avoid compulsory pregnancy, the enforced conception and bearing of unwanted children. If compulsory pregnancy is to be avoided, contraceptive services and voluntary abortion

[2] Larry Bumpass and Charles F. Westoff, "The 'perfect contraceptive' population," *Science* (vol. 169, 1970) pp. 1177-1182. Exactly how much the growth rate would be reduced is the subject of dispute and uncertainty. This should not, however, be allowed to prevent a concerted effort toward reducing the number of unwanted births.

should be available on demand to *all* American women.

Programs to provide accessibility to contraception and abortion are opposed by two classes of people. There are those who are against contraception and abortion on moral grounds. No one, of course, should be forced to use contraceptives or have an abortion. There is no reason to believe that population control in the United States cannot be achieved without such measures, and those opposed to contraception and abortion may personally avoid either or both. Unhappily, some people have wished to force their morality on others, preventing them by law from having access to contraception or abortion. Although most laws limiting the dissemination of contraceptive information and devices have been eliminated, many states still have restrictive abortion laws.

Restrictive abortion laws have one principal effect—to force women, particularly poor women, to seek unsafe abortions. The affluent have always had access to safe abortion, both at home and overseas. Even in some states with so-called "liberalized" abortion laws, the costs of abortion remain beyond most women. The time is overdue when *all* abortion laws should be struck down, to be replaced by a federal statute leaving decisions about abortions in the hands of the woman and her physician. It should be a felony for a doctor to refuse an abortion on any but medical grounds (with provision for referral if the doctor's personal morals will not permit him to recommend or perform the operation). Women must have control over what they may or may not do with their bodies.

A more serious barrier in the way of making contraception and abortion available to all is presented by a second group, those who fear that programs designed to be voluntary will turn out in practice to be coercive. The Congress may pass a bill setting up free contraception and abortion clinics in ghettos, but who is to guarantee that they will always be administered without coercion? The answer is that such guarantees are difficult to provide at the local level; "voluntary" programs may indeed become the basis for considerable pressure. Perhaps the best strategy is to design programs to be administered at the local level by people drawn from the local community. Black women in a ghetto should have access to contraception and safe abortion *if they want it*. But they should not have to seek such services from white men or women. Let black women run the clinics.

Another fear raised in connection with availability of contraception and abortion is embodied in the "first-step argument." The governor of one of our largest states recently said that, if abortion laws were further relaxed, the next step would be abortion one, two, or more months after birth (his limited vocabulary apparently did not include the term infanticide!). On a TV program dealing with the population problem, an agitated man opposed abortion as a step toward genocide because Hitler had forced Jewish women to have abortions. (Hitler also built autobahns but the man seemed relaxed about the federal highway program.) Of all religious groups in the United States, Jews are most in favor of liberalized abortion laws.

The "first-step argument" is familiar to anyone who has ever attempted to institute any reform. The only way to deal with it is to point out that anything can be carried too far, and that in many cases one step may be highly desirable and the succeeding one undesirable. Allowing people access to a service is not necessarily followed by forcing anyone to use it.

The federal government should be seeing to it that contraception and abortion are available to all who desire them. Some progress has been made in the direction of giving the poor access to contraceptives. Relatively comprehensive legislation to extend family planning to all Americans may well be passed early in the 1970's. The prospects for sane abortion legislation from Congress are considerably dimmer.

Beyond making family planning available, the government should also be taking the first steps in a *program of population control.* It is important that such programs be clearly differentiated from family planning. Family planning takes into consideration the needs of couples; population control considers the needs of everyone in the society.

Although at the moment the population size "needs" of American society have not been determined, we can be sure that any optimum will be well below the size of the present population. No one has yet presented a sound argument for having more than 150 million Americans. The only reason presented for having a number even that large is that we might need to fight another war demanding a large expenditure of manpower. We fought the largest land war in history, the Second World War, with fewer than 150 million Americans. As should be obvious from events such as the Arab-Israeli Six-Day War, brute manpower counts for considerably less today than it did at the time of World War II. Moreover, if we continue to plan to settle international arguments on Spaceship Earth with violence, we can be sure that our voyage will be short and unpleasant.

With a population of 205 million people, the United States seems to be unable to confer the "good life" on at least 30 million people. Americans would be well advised to ask themselves how we are going to deal with an additional 90 million persons or so in the next thirty years. At the moment, we tend to deny full membership in our society to blocks of people, not to individuals. Blacks, those who speak Spanish, and Appalachian and southern rural whites have been cut out. What additional groups will be cut out as the population grows? Would it not be better to stop population growth and rescue the present "outs"?

Since there already are more than enough people in the United States, we would choose to stop growth and extend the benefits of society to all Americans. Indeed, since the ability of our life-support systems to maintain themselves and us is inversely proportional to our population size, it is the *duty* of citizens and the government to bend every effort to halt our population growth and start a slow population decline. What must be done is to change the present pronatalist policies of our society and substitute antinatalist policies. We must create a social milieu in which families *want* fewer children. Women must be offered greater access to careers other than childrearing. Men must learn to be proud of the quality of their children, not their quantity. Society as a whole must come to consider remaining single or being married and childless as being constructive, satisfying modes of existence (trends in either direction should be self-reinforcing—the more single people or childless couples there are, the more acceptable it will be). The way for society to start this shift of attitude is, obviously, through its principal instrument for corporate action: the government.

Logically, the first effort in this direction should come from the Executive Branch. A courageous President would go before the American people and announce that the nation faced a severe crisis of overpopulation. He would briefly explain the nature of the crisis and the connection between overpopulation and environmental deterioration. He would point out that dramatic action is necessary *now*, if we are to preserve a livable world for our children. The built-in growth potential of our youthful population would be emphasized. The President would explain that, even if the average number of children born into each family from that moment on was only slightly over two, our population would continue to grow well into the next century.[3]

---

[3] When the average family size drops to the level which *eventually* will lead to a stable population size (zero population growth or ZPG), the population does not stop growing immediately. Even if we should reach by 1980 a reproductive rate at which each adult female alive was replaced by exactly one adult female in the next generation, population growth would continue until 2045. The population when growth stopped would be over 300 million. For the demographic details see Tomas Frejka, "Reflections on the demographic conditions needed to establish a U.S. stationary population growth," *Population Studies*, vol. 22, pp. 379-397, 1968.

The President might emphasize that even a successful population control program would not bring swift results, but would provide immeasurable benefits to our children. He would plead with Americans to give women full rights in our society and for men to assume a larger role in limiting family size. He could close his speech by appealing for every patriotic, responsible American couple to limit themselves to producing an absolute maximum of two children, pointing out that if we cannot control our population size with voluntary methods the government will be forced to take further action.

The President might then begin to put pressure on various executive agencies to create a milieu in which small family size would be a national ideal. Perhaps the most important role would be played by the Federal Communications Commission (FCC), which could require TV and radio stations to give abundant free air time to spot "commercials" about the population crisis.

What might they be like? One might start with a view of the smoggy hell of Los Angeles with a graph indicating the skyrocketing emphysema death rate superimposed. Quickly cut to an empty school yard with a standard smog-alert message, "Don't let the children run and play" heard in the background. Then cut to a clogged freeway, with the voice message in the background, "Los Angeles has a fatal disease: overpopulation." Another spot might show a woman with a large family scraping dirty diapers and muttering, "Now they tell me that children from large families don't do as well as those from small families. And with six screaming kids what chance do I have to be a satisfied human being. . . ."

The FCC could also ban all commercials and programing which showed families with more than two children in a positive light, and could encourage programing which portrayed childless couples as having a full life and making valuable contributions to society. Similarly, single people of both sexes could be presented as symbols of virility or femininity on other bases besides fatherhood or motherhood.

The National Institute of Health could give substantial grants for the development of such commercials. The CAB could restrict airlines to providing "family plan" benefits to a maximum of two natural children, and promote special rates for unmarried people, childless couples, and adopted children. All departments and agencies could see to it that only small families are portrayed attractively in their literature.

The President would order the Census Bureau to run a series of extra-detailed sample census and attitude surveys over a period of two years to see whether or not the propaganda effort of the Executive Branch was having the desired effect. If the reproductive rate were dropping satisfactorily, no further effort would be made except to continue careful monitoring of the demographic situation. The government's propaganda efforts could then be adjusted to produce whatever birthrate was deemed desirable, taking into account the age structure of the population (number of women in their reproductive years, etc.).

If, on the other hand, birthrates did not drop sufficiently, further governmental action would be required. Presumably the least objectionable approach would be an incentive system designed to discourage or delay the beginning of childbearing. One suggestion has been that a bonus be given each woman for every year between the ages of 15 and 28 that she does not have her first child—say $500.[4] Similar possibilities include payment of such bonuses to women who do not produce a third child when they were between the ages of 25 and 50 or

---

[4] Delaying the onset of childbearing is an effective way to slow or halt population growth. It might also have social advantages in encouraging more stable family units. It has the disadvantage, however, of promoting reproduction by older women who are more likely to produce children with birth defects. As is often the case, a careful weighing of potential social costs and benefits should precede a decision to institute such a program.

large bonuses for sterilization after the second child is born.

In the long run, such a program would save the taxpayers a considerable amount of money, since population growth is now an extremely expensive proposition. We are already far past the point where adding more people saves money for each person. We have largely exhausted the possibilities for "economies of scale" in production of goods, transportation systems, and so on. Now we are faced with higher costs per individual as population grows—with "diseconomies of scale." The more people there are, the more scarce and inaccessible are the resources that must be exploited and the greater the expense of cleaning up the environment. For instance, as city after city is discovering, straightforward "dump it and forget it" sewage and garbage disposal techniques will not suffice for large populations. A larger and larger per-person expenditure is required as the population grows and the natural capacity of the environment to recycle wastes is exhausted. The list of diseconomies of scale associated with overpopulation is very long.

As Professor K. E. F. Watt has pointed out,[5] population growth produces an increased burden on each individual taxpayer. A growing population is a young population. There are proportionately more people in the ages benefiting from education taxes than in those producing tax revenues. The highest crime rates also occur in the 16–24 age bracket, so that the costs of police protection will also tend to be higher in a growing population. Watt estimates, "if the rate of population increase goes up from no increase to just 1 percent per annum, this means that the tax burden per taxpayer is 25 percent higher than it would have been if the population was not growing." He estimates that if the rate jumps from zero growth to 3 percent, the burden per taxpayer for educa-

---

[5] "Whole Earth," in *Earth Day, the Beginning* (New York: Arno Press/New York Times, 1970), pp. 6–7.

tion taxes alone will treble. As Professor Watt observes, few people realize "the amazing sensitivity of the tax burden to very small changes in the rate of population increase." Therefore, though it might be difficult to find the money for an incentive program initially, it would more than pay for itself in the long run.

There is, however, one major potential difficulty with such a program. It would tend to discriminate against the poor. And because a greater proportion of the people in minority groups are poor, the program would discriminate against minorities. After all, how many affluent women would allow a $500 bonus to dissuade them from having a child they wanted? The main impact of such a program on the affluent would be in making crystal clear the point that the government considered overreproduction irresponsible.

A less discriminatory and therefore potentially more effective program might be simply to cut the income tax in half for each woman for each year she did not reproduce, with a similar tax break going to guardians of girls who do not pay taxes. Since most of the poor have little or no income tax liability, the system would discriminate against the prime villains: the middle class. The effect on the rich, however, would probably be negligible, since the present tax structure is largely a swindle perpetrated by the rich at the expense of the middle class and poor.[6] Replacement of our regressive income tax system with a truly progressive one would help in this area as well as in many others.

Once some sort of incentive system had been established, the results would again be carefully monitored. A satisfactory decline in birth rates would almost certainly result. If, however, the desired results were not achieved, more stringent measures would be called for.

---

[6] Ferdinand Lundberg writes, "The national tax burden is largely shouldered, absolutely and relatively, by the politically illiterate nonmanagerial labor force rather than by big property owners or by upper-echelon corporate executives (who are often tax free.)"—*The Rich and the Super-Rich*, p. 389.

This could mean a series of heavy taxes on parents with many children. A tax system could be designed to avoid adding to the burdens of the poor and thus avoid penalizing children instead of parents. This could be done by careful setting of minimum income standards after taxes. Since having too many children places an enormous burden on society and reduces the survival chances of any individual child, it is only proper that overbreeders *with money for luxuries* pay through the nose.

If all else failed, the government would eventually place criminal sanctions on overbreeding. The prospect of an already inept, inefficient and sometimes corrupt federal establishment moving directly into the reproductive lives of Americans can be viewed only with horror. Furthermore, one might argue that the government is so slow to respond to environmental change that such a positive reaction to the problem would be a sign that it was already much too late. However, those who claim that the government could never intrude into such a private matter as the number of children a couple produces may be due for an unpleasant surprise. There is no sacred legal "right" to have children. The argument that family size is God's affair and not the business of the government would undoubtedly be raised—just as it was against outlawing polygamy. But the government tells you precisely how many husbands or wives you can have and claps you in jail if you exceed that number. Having a third child (except as one of a multiple birth) may some day produce the same unhappy result—unless we manage to stem the tide of population voluntarily.

Let us make the not illogical assumption that a courageous President's pushing a change in attitudes toward family size will result in a dramatic drop in the birth rate. Suppose the *average* completed family dropped to *less* than two children, giving us a chance to halt population growth in the United States by early in the next century (this does not necessarily mean there would be no large families, just that proportionately many more people would have no children or only one child). What would be the consequences of such a triumph?

The most obvious would be a change in the age structure of the population. The numbers of the young would decrease, and there would be proportionately more old people. The average age of the population would increase. This increase in the average age has been the basis of what is perhaps the most preposterous argument against population control. After all, it is argued, old folks tend to be conservative (and therefore undesirable?), and, if we control our population, there will be more old folks. Of course, even people who would be silly enough to use this argument realize that population growth cannot continue forever, and that whenever growth is halted an increase in the average age of the population is a mathematical certainty. But they would like to defer this problem so that our descendants can wrestle with it in an even more overpopulated world!

A few minutes' consideration will make it clear that the population-aging "problem" rather than being a reason for not controlling our numbers is itself a symptom of the sickening of our society, a symptom not unconnected with overpopulation.[7] Is the "conservatism" of our older citizens an unavoidable biological consequence of being old? Perhaps the troubles of our aged are to a great degree a product of the way our society functions. First of all, Americans firmly believe that their most important activities are those connected with their work, with their economic lives. However, the number of people who can lead useful economic lives in our society is becoming increasingly limited in the face of automation. Indeed, almost one half of our labor force may already be victims of disguised unemployment, working at jobs which are useless or could be done better by machine. The glut of labor is made worse by

---

[7] A related symptom of the youth cult. Why should persons under 21 find airline space available at one-half price when they want to go skiing while older people wanting to visit their grandchildren cannot?

the large numbers of young people generated by our population growth, young people who must find their own economic ladders to climb. A prime result of this labor glut is compulsory retirement. Older people must be ejected from the labor force to make room for the youngsters moving in.

One might think that early retirement would be a blessing. But it is not. Outside of their economic lives, many, if not most, Americans have few interests or resources. Leisure to read, write, or contemplate is not high on their lists of goals. Their lives have revolved around making a buck so they could buy all those trinkets the TV hucksters dangle before them. In retirement they are denied even the pleasure of making money. In our super-mobile society they probably have little or no contact with their families, especially their children and grandchildren. They are shunted off into old-age ghettos, to spin out their lives with hobbies (if they are fortunate) or just sitting and staring at TV. Small wonder we have conservative oldsters. What other choice do they have?

We could, of course, restructure our society so that, rather than swelling the ranks of the John Birch Society, our old folks become interested, active, informed, and happy. The very process of stopping population growth would be a start in the right direction. As the ranks of the very young dwindled, the need for allocating huge amounts of money to public school systems would abate. More money would be available to help with the problems of older people, and it would be easier for them to remain in their economic roles longer.

Perhaps most important, society could afford to establish a continuing education system in which people could be given leave from their jobs every seventh year (as sabbatical leaves are now given to many teachers). These leaves could be used to return to school, or simply for individual study and refreshment. If the program were properly designed and operated, the result would be a much higher quality of population at all ages. Surely one of the silliest ideas of our society is that education is best delivered in a massive and continuous dose during the first quarter century of life. There are good reasons for interrupting education during the so-called formative years, and equally good reasons for continuing it later. With effort, we should be able to create a society with swinging old people, old people who play an active role as they do in most human societies. And with continuing education we could convert all Americans into crew members of Spaceship Earth, rather than have most of them exist in the passive role of passengers.

Population Control in Other ODCs

If the record of the United States government in the areas of both population control and the maintenance of environmental quality is abysmal, the records of most other ODCs are worse. Many other ODCs, such as England, Canada, and Australia, still *encourage* reproduction with family allowances. In countries like Canada and Australia the primitive notion that people per square mile is the critical measure of population pressure prevails. Indeed, both of these countries fail to realize that at best they are just short of being overpopulated. Their numbers are even now beginning to press on both their resources and their values. The Soviet Union has unhappily also failed to recognize the threat of overpopulation. The Soviets are insanely pressing for *higher* birth rates. "Mother Heroine of the Soviet Union" medals are still conferred upon women who bear five or more children.

In the most heavily overpopulated countries of Western Europe, the situation is generally worse. Few Europeans seem to realize that they must draw heavily on the rest of the world for the resources necessary to maintain their affluence. Few also seem to realize that, with a few exceptions, European nations could not feed themselves without importing food (or fertilizer, or the petroleum to run farm machinery, etc.). A Dane once bragged to me about his nation's position as a food exporter, sending dairy products, eggs, and meat to other nations. He was not aware that, in order to do so, Denmark has to import vast amounts of protein, much of it in the form of oilseed cakes and grain to be fed to livestock. More protein is imported, per person, by Denmark than by any other nation in the world. For each Danish man, woman, and child, 240 pounds of protein enter the country, nearly three times the average protein consumption of each Dane. The Netherlands is the second largest per capita protein importer at 170 pounds.[8]

Even an island nation like Great Britain seems relatively oblivious to her extreme degree of overpopulation. At a recent conference on "Optimum Population in Britain," one distinguished participant pointed out that only a small percentage of England was used by man (the significance of the green fields of England's countryside was lost on him—after all, people weren't standing in them, *ergo* they were not "used"!) The fact of Great Britain's almost total dependence on the rest of the world is only dimly perceived, and the continuance of today's world trade system is simply taken for granted. Great Britain's recent adoption of a liberalized

---

[8] The uninitiated often point to the Netherlands, with its population density some 15 times that of the U.S.A., as an example to show that the United States is underpopulated. Of course, a much greater percentage of the Netherlands than of the U.S. is arable, but this is not the essence of the fallacy. The Netherlands is not remotely self-sufficient. It imports about 50% of its wheat, 100% of its rice, 75% of its other cereals, *all* of its steel, antimony, bauxite, chromium, copper, gold, lead, magnesite, manganese, mercury, molybdenum, nickel, silver, tin, tungsten, vanadium, zinc, phosphate rock (fertilizer), potash (fertilizer), asbestos, and diamonds. It produces the energy equivalent of some 20 million metric tons of coal and consumes the equivalent of over 47 million metric tons. Obviously, the Dutch do not live off the 15,800 square miles of the Netherlands— vast amounts of land elsewhere on the Earth are dedicated to their support. (Sources: Borgstrom, *Too Many*, p. 238; *U.N. Statistical Yearbook*, 1968).

policy toward abortion seems to be motivated largely by humanitarian considerations rather than an awareness of her gross state of overpopulation.

Lack of concern for overpopulation can be traced to ignorance in many Western European nations, as well as to persistent though repeatedly discredited ideas of strength through numbers. In a continent so often racked by wars it is perhaps understandable that people do not want to be outnumbered by their neighbors. However, one would think that Napoleon's and Hitler's successes against vastly larger populations and, more recently, the victory of the Israelis over the Arabs would finally have put to death the notion that sheer numbers provide military security.

Another factor in attitudes toward overpopulation in some nations may be the position of the hierarchy of the Roman Catholic Church. But it seems unlikely that this influence is great, since birth rates in Catholic nations such as Italy are comparable to those of economically similar non-Catholic nations. Abortion thrives in Catholic nations, and overt opposition to the antique views of the Pope and Curia is expressed in very high levels of the hierarchy, with open rebellion at the lower levels.

Birth rates also tend to be low in Eastern Europe and the Soviet Union where a religious dogma on population quite similar to that of official Catholicism holds sway. Indeed, the writings of old-line Catholic economists such as Colin Clark often have the same flavor as those of Communist demographers such as M. M. Sokolov of the Soviet Union. The population position of the modern Marxists is especially pathetic. Their reasoning is characteristic of latter-day followers of historic genuises. Modern Marxists assume that Karl Marx, if he were alive today, would have the same position on population today as he had in the middle of the last century. Nothing seems more unlikely. Karl Marx was a revolutionary, but he was first an intellectual. He did not spend years of his life in the reading room of the British Museum in order to avoid new ideas. Indeed, he often took note of mistakes in his earlier writings and discussed them in later writings. (For example, he noted in *Das Kapital* that his earlier thesis that the number of capitalists would decrease was contradicted by statistics showing the number actually increasing.) It is preposterous to assume that such a learned man would remain ignorant of the role of overpopulation in destroying Spaceship Earth, as do many today who call themselves Marxists.

Marx's reaction to Malthus, who first warned of the dangers of overpopulation, was so violent that, as William Petersen suggests, his constant hyperbole suggested a polemical weakness because "vituperation is no more a sign of strength with Marx than with any other social analyst." Marx himself pointed out that, if Malthus were correct, the "iron law of wages" (that wages tended to stabilize at minimum subsistence level) could not be circumvented, that "Socialism cannot abolish poverty, which is based on nature, but only *communalize* it, distribute it equally over the whole surface of society." [9] The "iron law" has long since been shown not to hold, at least in ODCs, but Marx's antipathy to Malthus still influences many people who ought to know better. Even in nominally Marxist nations, there is a growing realization that the population problem is not simply an attempt by "Malthusians" to conceal the ills of society (social injustice, maldistribution, etc.) behind a claim of "too many people."

In spite of officially pro-natalist policies, the Communist countries of Eastern Europe and the Soviet Union provide both contraceptive services and abortion through their health services. Relatively low birth rates in these countries may be traced also to the discouragement of early marriage and to an emphasis on women's playing roles other than that of mother. Education and full outside employment of women are generally en-

---

[9] *Critique of the Gotha Program* (New York: International Publishers, 1933), p. 40.

couraged, and child-care facilities are often provided to permit women to pursue careers.

There is one really bright light in an otherwise generally dismal picture of population awareness in Europe. Sweden has developed an extensive program of sex education for her schools, a program in which discussion of birth control is included. Family planning is included in the national health organization, and there is a relatively liberal policy on abortion. Although awareness of Sweden's own overpopulation is probably low, she has led all other ODCs in giving foreign aid in the area of population control.

Japan is in many ways a unique case among the ODCs. After her failure in the early 1940's to obtain a resource base which she deemed appropriate for her ambitions of growth, Japan came face to face with reality. After World War II, instead of occupying and drawing on the riches of a "Greater East Asia Co-prosperity Sphere" the Japanese people were left with dominion over considerably less territory than they had had at the start of the war. There was no way for the populace to fool themselves with the kinds of nonsense people in ODCs often use to avoid facing the facts of overpopulation. There was no empty land which could theoretically be cultivated, and agriculture was already very efficient. Japan was already overcrowded and heavily dependent on imports, and the Japanese knew it.

Supported by strong popular sentiment, Japan's abortion laws were liberalized and as a result the birth rate dropped by some 50 per cent. Subsequently, increased use of contraceptives has reduced the abortion rate without permitting the birth rate to increase. In 1970 however, Japan was growing as fast or faster than the U.S.A., U.S.S.R., and all the major nations of Europe except Rumania. Although she once had a fighting chance to bring that rate to zero and to start the slow population decline necessary for her survival, that chance now seems to have gone by the board. Industry, frightened by the prospect of "cheap labor" competition

THE SIZE OF THE CREW

from Hong Kong and elsewhere, withdrew its support from the population control program. And recently, the Japanese Prime Minister Eisako Sato advocated an increase in Japan's birthrate to help "solve" the labor shortage problem.

As economist Alan R. Sweezey has pointed out,[10] this particular bit of government idiocy is due to a "failure to distinguish between per capita and overall expansion." A growing labor force will permit Japan's total gross national product (GNP) to increase more rapidly than it will if the size of the labor force remains constant. But increase in *per capita* GNP will be more likely if the labor force is small in relation to the amount of available capital. As Sweezey says, "The case for considering per capita rather than total GNP is especially strong in a country like Japan where overcrowding is already acute and where the negative effects of expansion on the quality of life, which are not included in the conventional measure of GNP, are in consequence especially large." Amen!

What can be done to institute population control among the other ODCs? Obviously a great hope is rapid public education. People in these countries must be made aware of the origins of the food and other resources they consume and the part played by overpopulation in their increasingly serious pollution problems. Above all, they, like the citizens of the United States, must become aware of their dependence on the life-support systems and the other passengers on Spaceship Earth.

There are some signs of such awakening, but all too few. There is some small hope that the United Nations conference on the environment in 1972 will make more ODC citizens aware of their overpopulation problems, but we doubt it. Among other things, a combination of Catholic and Marxist elements will probably play down the population component in the environmental crisis.

---

[10] *Science*, July 3, 1970, p. 97.

Perhaps the best Americans can hope for is that, by establishing and publicizing strong population policies in the U.S., they can set an example which will greatly aid those in the other ODCs with the intelligence and breadth of vision to recognize their own problems. We are convinced that population control can be achieved in the other ODCs, and by methods analogous to those already discussed for the U.S.A. But, just as in the U.S.A., the problem must be apprehended by a substantial proportion of the population before it can be solved. Awakening the citizens of the ODCs will be one of the more difficult tasks in saving our Ship.

Population Control in UDCs

Nobody stands to gain more rapidly from population control than do the people of the UDCs. At the moment a major problem in all of these rapidly growing countries is their high dependency loads. Because they are growing so rapidly, they have a large number of dependent, nonproductive children in proportion to the number of people in their work force. Characteristically, between 40 and 45 per cent of the population of UDCs is under 15 years of age. Because of this large proportion of young people, it will take a long time for population growth to stop, *even if the size of completed families drops dramatically*. That is, in the happy event that a birth control revolution should occur in the UDCs, they will continue to grow rapidly until well into the next century. The reason is that the huge mass of young people now born will have children *and* grandchildren in the 50 years it will take for them to move from ages 0-15 to ages 50-65. And, barring disaster, today's mass of young people will not contribute heavily to the death side of the birth-death equation until they move into those years when the diseases of aging take their toll.

Why then, if this population control inertia is built

into the age structure of the population, should the UDCs derive such rapid benefits from population control? The answer lies again in the age structure. The effects of reduced birth rates obviously show up first at the bottom of the age scale. The number of infants is reduced, which soon leads to a reduction in the number of young people. The age classes of the population that shrink *first* in response to population control *are those which are currently responsible for the high dependency load*. Therefore, an effective birth control program will raise the standard of living in a country almost immediately by decreasing the unproductive portion of the population.

No competent social or natural scientist doubts the enormous benefits to be gained by UDCs through rigorous population control measures. These scientists are horrified by the prospective consequences of continued growth—incredible levels of unemployment, increasing inequality (a growing gap between economic classes), rapid growth of slum-filled cities, economic regression, declining public health, increasing starvation, and destruction of ecological systems, to name a few. Some governments in the UDCs have recognized the critical negative role played by overpopulation in their national development and have moved to curtail population growth. Most noteworthy among the larger countries have been India, Pakistan, and the People's Republic of China.

India has the longest history of attempted population control. Her first national family planning program was initiated in 1952, when the birth rate was 40 per thousand and the death rate 27 per thousand. Although the program was reorganized and greatly expanded in 1965, it has been a complete failure. In 1970 India's birth rate was 42 per thousand, slightly *higher* than it was in 1952, her death rate only 17 per thousand. Her population was growing fast enough to double every 27 years, in contrast to the 1952 rate which would have doubled the population every 53 years.

The reasons for India's failure give us some insight into what will be necessary if population control is to succeed in UDCs. One of India's main problems has been, of course, logistic. Simply assembling the transport and training and organizing personnel to bring birth control techniques into some one half million villages was an enormous task. The task was made even more difficult by the policy of promoting birth control exclusively in a context of Western medicine. This has caused resentment among practitioners of India's three other active medical traditions—homeopathic, ayurvedic, and unani. This resentment has greatly limited the adoption of birth control techniques, since Western medicine reaches primarily better educated people (especially in the cities), a group that makes up a relatively insignificant portion of the population. In some villages family planning teams have even met with outright hostility, and riots leading to the destruction of team camps and mobile equipment have resulted.

Other difficulties have been connected with birth control techniques themselves. Little progress was made at first in promoting vasectomies (the simple male sterilization operation). Then it was recognized that a major difficulty was the performing of the operation in hospitals. Most Indians thought of hospitals as a place one went to die—hardly a factor to encourage prospective vasectomy customers. Vasectomy clinics have now been opened in railroad stations, with more hopeful results. India's earliest attempts at family planning involved the use of the rhythm method, a notoriously failure-prone technique even when practiced by highly educated and highly motivated people. Condoms were also tried but with little success. They are relatively effective when used properly, but also require high motivation, since they must be used each time intercourse occurs. In addition, assuming they are only used once each, the supply problem can be monumental, with perhaps 50 million required *daily* in India alone.

Intrauterine devices (IUDs) seemed to hold more promise. These plastic loops inserted into the uterus are, if retained, very effective at preventing conception. They have the enormous advantage of requiring no day-to-day motivation. In addition they are cheap (the device costs only a few cents and may be retained for years), and can be inserted by paramedical personnel with relatively little training.

Unfortunately, the IUD did not turn out to be the expected panacea in India. In many women it causes side effects, including discomfort and bleeding, especially increased menstrual bleeding. The bleeding is especially likely to occur in malnourished women, and a substantial number of women in India (and in other UDCs) are malnourished. In addition to these unpleasant side-effects, a series of rumors were circulated about the IUD. It was supposed to make copulating couples stick together or to shock the man during intercourse. It was rumored that it would migrate through the bloodstream and enter the brain. The popularity of the IUD, which was relatively high initially, soon plummeted and has not been restored.

A final problem in India (and other UDCs) is the rampant corruption characteristic of "soft states" as Gunnar Myrdal calls them.[11] It makes implementation of programs difficult and expensive, and evaluation of programs all but impossible. An official may brag about how many condoms have been distributed, but neglect to mention, as one person put it, that the majority were used as flashlight covers. Most statistics originating in UDCs are highly suspect, and there can be little doubt that the "success" of family planning operations is generally inflated in reports. This is especially true where

[11] See Gunnar Myrdal, *The Challenge of World Poverty* (New York: Pantheon, 1970). Also, Bernard Nossiter's *The Soft State: A Newspaperman's Chronicle of India* (New York: Harper & Row, 1970) has a most interesting discussion of the problems of population control in India.

"bounties" are paid for recruiting people for vasectomies.

We can summarize the needs of population control programs in UDCs rather easily. They include:

1. Education to change the attitudes of leaders.

2. Education to change the attitudes of the mass of the people.

3. Satisfactory birth control technology.

4. Logistic support for dissemination of technology.

5. Effective systems of program evaluation.

Educating Leaders. The need to educate leaders on the necessity for population control is not universal. In India, Pakistan, and China the need seems to be firmly recognized by at least part of the leadership, as it is by many leaders in some smaller Asiatic countries such as Singapore and South Korea. Nevertheless, in most UDCs, especially in Africa and Latin America, leaders tend to be as ignorant about the need for population control as are their colleagues in the ODCs. In part this can be traced to their education, which, perhaps even more than that of ODC leaders, has been deficient in areas such as ecology and agriculture. Some of these nations have relatively low population densities, and their leadership makes the elementary error of using people per square mile as their standard of underpopulation or overpopulation.

It is clearly too late for any change in the education systems of UDCs to influence those leaders who will be making decisions in the critical decade of the 1970's. The best hope for changing opinions in this group lies, first, in the ODCs setting an example and, second, in strong leadership from the United Nations. In the latter case, a great deal will depend on the success that educated Catholics have in the next year or so in changing the unfortunate views of Pope and Curia on birth control. Rank and file Catholics in most nations tend to behave reproductively much as their non-Catholic cohorts do. (There is some tendency for people to express their anti-Catholic bias by saying that the population problem is a Catholic problem. This is nonsense.) Unfortunately, however, in some Catholic countries the position of the hierarchy has some influence on government, which has led (as we have noted before) to collaboration with the Communists in blocking effective population crisis propaganda or population control measures by U.N. agencies. But the tide in this battle seems to be turning, and we can hope that humanitarian forces within the church will soon present mankind with a major victory.

There is, of course, a sad but powerful force working toward changing the views of both leaders and citizens all over the world relative to population control. As population growth continues unabated, the world situation will continue to deteriorate. This will undoubtedly quicken the conversion to population control policies among those governments which have a genuine interest in the welfare of their people. Other UDC governments concerned primarily with the maintenance of the status quo (and especially of the position of the ruling oligarchy) hopefully will disappear as conditions worsen. Whether or not this happens will depend in no small degree on whether the United States can learn enough from the Indochina fiasco to establish a new, realistic foreign policy which does not involve the support of such governments.

Educating the People. Once governments are convinced of the need for population control, the enormous problems of converting the general populace to that goal may be tackled. Education through the established school systems is part of the long-term answer, but badly needed reforms cannot be accomplished in the UDC school systems with the necessary speed. In the UDCs even more than in the ODCs, however, there is the need for the development of first-class education systems (eventually all human beings should have access to continuing education throughout their lives). Therefore one of the first steps in a population control program in the UDCs would be the establishment of a broad adult education program. Such a program would not merely teach about the need for and techniques of birth control, it would also help raise literacy levels, give advice on ecologically sound farming, and in general be a major weapon in the struggle for semi-development (see chapter 5).

How could such a program be initiated? This is an area where ODC aid, carefully managed and unobtrusive, may be of immense assistance. Before discussing educational or other programs in which the ODCs aid the UDCs, a caveat is necessary. Any such programs must be guarded against the twin threats of bureaucratic inertia and careerism. For instance, once an official has been working on a program for a few years and inevitably making decisions on the basis of inadequate data, it will become very difficult for him to face up to a failure of the program. Even if he *knows* it is failing, interorganizational politics will force him to defend it. Perhaps the best way to avoid this would be to have permanent staff limited to housekeeping functions and to recruit professionals on a basis of three-year, nonrenewable terms. What is lost in continuity would be a small price to pay for retaining flexibility. Ad hoc review panels could also be employed liberally for frequent program evaluation.

Another major need in the UDCs is for channels of communication. These could be established with present technology by supplying villages with battery or generator powered, single channel TV sets for communal viewing. Funds for such a project could be made available by a reallocation of resources by ODCs, resources now squandered on space flights, MIRVs, and the like. The problem of how properly to use a nationwide educational TV network in a UDC is much more complex. Programming will have to be designed with great care by people with intimate knowledge of local conditions. Unfortunately, the needed social scientists have not been trained, and school systems in neither UDCs nor ODCs are designed to produce them. Therefore another requirement for solving the population control problems of the UDCs (and many other of their problems) is a crash program of establishing centers for training technical personnel. These centers should be set up wherever possible in the UDCs with aid from the ODCs. There is in at least some UDCs a ready supply of "educated" persons who could be trained to perform the required tasks. In these countries higher education is available primarily to the children of the elite, and the tertiary schools "continued to produce an oversupply of 'generalists' . . . who swell the ranks of . . . the 'educated unemployed.' "[12] The UDCs are oversupplied with lawyers, poets, and academic scientists, and undersupplied with teachers, agriculturalists, engineers, physicians, and the like.

With the proper incentives, many of these people might be rapidly retrained to play vital roles in population control programs and other essential aspects of semi-development. The lack of suitable employment in UDCs for many of their highly trained citizens should work to the benefit of such a program. Operating against it is a snobbery which exceeds even that found among the educated of the ODCs, on whose systems UDC systems are modeled. One reason that ODC agriculture is an ecological disaster area is the snobbery of academic biologists who allowed the "non-pure" science of agriculture to be isolated in special institutions, where it suffered from lack of contact with the mainstream of

[12] Myrdal, *The Challenge of World Poverty*, p. 192.

biology. Even today, with humanity facing a vast food crisis, few graduates of ODC universities know the first thing about agriculture, and many academic biologists look down their noses at the "applied" problems of agriculture.

The necessary change of attitude among the "educated unemployed" of the UDCs can be facilitated by dramatic changes of priorities in ODCs. If a substantial number of distinguished ODC scientists began to devote time to the "applied" problems of the world, the prestige gradient in the minds of UDC scientists would begin to change. The ODCs could also take a very simple step that would help UDCs to build the educated cadres they require. All student visas for UDC citizens should be strictly temporary so that trained people would be required to return to their native lands. Migration of educated people from UDCs to ODCs should also be discouraged.

The aim of all this is, of course, to provide the people to analyze the routes to population control in a given country and to design the educational programs which will start people along those routes. If, for instance, Indian villagers had been exposed to TV programs about the need for population control, programs which included lectures by practitioners of all medical traditions, the job of the birth control field teams would undoubtedly have been eased. Equally, women could have been prepared for the side effects of IUDs before they were introduced, perhaps preventing much of the difficulty with that program. The nature of vasectomy could have been clearly explained, so that men would not have confused it with castration.

A potential criticism of such communications programing is that it may cause distress and disturbance because "such things are simply not discussed in public." This sort of problem is precisely what the trained social scientists will attempt to circumvent. Nevertheless, it would be fatuous to assume that all disruption can be avoided when promoting a social revolution. Cultures will have to be changed because fundamental attitudes of the people within the culture will be changed. It is probable, however, that the amount of disruption accompanying the introduction of population control would be minor in comparison with that resulting even now from overpopulation.

It must be emphasized that in many areas attempts to change attitudes in order to achieve population control will involve a great deal of effort in addition to, or instead of, describing the problems of overpopulation and promoting birth control techniques. In many cases, efforts should undoubtedly be made to change the traditional role of women in society, encouraging them to leave the home and participate more fully in the economic life of society. This may involve, for instance, the building of day-care centers for children. The interrelatedness of the problems of semi-development is illustrated by one of the dangers of taking this course. One of the great problems of the UDCs is unemployment. Adding women to the labor force will only exacerbate this problem unless unemployment is attacked systematically at the same time.

Perhaps the best initial roles for women in UDCs would be as teachers, agricultural technicians, and physicians or paramedical personnel. As noted above, these roles are often avoided by educated men. Educating women in these areas and establishing them in careers would tend directly to reduce the birth rate in the country, while simultaneously producing desirable feedback effects on other features of society necessary for semi-development. The effects might well be synergistic. Better educated people would be more likely to grasp the problems of overpopulation and their own increased chances for affluence with a smaller family.

Better educated people and more physicians and paramedical personnel would also result in higher standards of public health. A more efficient agricultural system, helped along by numerous female technicians, would also produce higher standards of public health, since malnutrition is the most serious disease in the UDCs. Higher standards of public health would reduce infant mortality. And, in the opinion of many observers, lowered infant and child mortalities will help reduce birth rates. Presumably when they are assured that their children will have a good chance of surviving to maturity, people will choose to have fewer children. Whether this effect will more than compensate demographically for lowered infant and child mortality is not known, it is merely assumed. It seems logical, however, to believe that women will be more willing to leave their traditional role of continual childbearing and choose careers for themselves if they are reasonably sure that the one or two children they do have will survive.

Improved public health should be coupled with a general drive toward increased "social security." In many UDCs parents depend on children for support in their old age. With high mortality rates among youngsters, people tend to have more children in order to be assured that some will survive to support them in old age. UDCs should develop mechanisms to assure the security of the aged as they work to reduce infant and child mortality rates.

There are many other reasons, in addition, why improved public health is essential to successful semi-development, and we will discuss them below. However, even if it were not, we must here make explicit a moral assumption which we consider to be a fundamental rule for the successful running of Spaceship Earth. "Solutions" to problems that deliberately increase the rate of suffering or death of any portion of humanity are unacceptable. The population problem cannot be "solved" by withholding medical services or food and letting people die of disease or starvation. The problems of land reform cannot be "solved" by shooting either the landlords or the landless.

We have let conditions on our spaceship deteriorate

to the point where mankind inevitably will face much suffering and many difficult decisions of resource allocation. But, in our opinion, all decisions must be made in a context of providing the best possible life for those people already on the Ship. The present death rate from starvation and the inevitably higher future death rates are not blessings, helping to reduce overpopulation. They are hideous consequences of man's stupidity and avarice—consequences which could have been avoided if programs of population control and equitable distribution of resources had been instituted in the middle of the twentieth century. Every effort must be bent to keep the death rate down as the birth rate is reduced, so that mankind as a whole can enjoy the fruits of a long life; every effort, that is, short of those so ecologically disruptive as to threaten the integrity of the life-support systems of our spacecraft and thus imperil everyone.

Birth Control Technology. The need for a more satisfactory birth control technology is apparent from the history of family planning efforts in the UDCs and elsewhere. Techniques are needed which minimize both undesirable side-effects and the amount of effort required for their use, and which will reduce the frequency of unwanted pregnancies virtually to zero. Finding, testing, and distributing such contraceptives should be a top priority goal of the research establishments of the ODCs. In the United States the death grip of the Food and Drug Administration (FDA) on contraceptive testing should be loosened to permit more rapid progress. As Dr. Carl Djerassi recently stated, we are "faced with the ironic situation that in . . . advanced nations, in which tobacco and alcohol sales are not restricted in spite of the serious 'side effects' of these agents, new candidates for contraceptive agents must meet much more rigorous standards than most other drugs." [18]

---

[18] Carl Djerassi. 1969. "Prognosis for the development of new chemical birth control agents," *Science* 166: 468-473. This article is a "must" for those interested in the problems of producing new contraceptives.

Some promising results have been produced with providing women with low, continuous doses of the hormone progestin. Such doses may be supplied by time capsules made of Silastic, a silicone rubber. These capsules can be designed for implantation under the skin through a hypodermic needle and, at least in theory, could provide protection for up to 30 years. Naturally, long-term testing will be required before we can be sure of the safety of such an implant or, for that matter, for any similar new contraceptive with unknown side effects. But, as Dr. Djerassi notes, if a crash program were developed the risks involved in testing could be much reduced. Above all, OCDs must develop contraceptives which are considered safe for their own populations; UDCs will not adopt measures that are "not good enough" for their overdeveloped friends.

There are other promising leads for new contraceptives, including a possible "morning after" pill, and the potentialities of contraceptives where the burden falls on the male have not been thoroughly explored. Nevertheless, in the crucial decade of the 1970's, it seems likely that worldwide population control efforts will probably be based largely on the present arsenal of contraceptives, plus vasectomy and abortion. Considerable improvement in technique has recently greatly increased the chances of restoring fertility to a man with a vasectomy. This removes one of the major psychological barriers to vasectomy—its "permanence" (we say "psychological" barriers because, in practice, there are virtually no requests for reversal of sterilization).

There have also been major strides in increasing the ease and safety of abortion, which is the most common form of birth control practiced worldwide. Soviet scientists have developed a new vacuum device which obviates the necessity of scraping the uterus (curettage). Their device has been widely adopted in Eastern Europe and has been introduced in the United States. Great steps have been taken recently in the United

States toward making medically performed abortions available to all women, but we still have a long way to go. In most of the rest of the world (Communist countries and Japan being the major exceptions) the situation remains grim. An assortment of taboos promoted by the men who dominate these cultures keep women from access to safe abortion. Thousands of women die annually from incompetent and unsanitary abortions—murdered in large part because of the superstitious beliefs of the opposite sex. There is no stronger argument for the liberation of women than the world abortion situation. Until truly satisfactory contraceptive methods are developed, we must have safe abortion available as a backup.

Logistic Support. ODCs should, of course, supply a great deal of logistic support for population control programs in the UDCs. Obviously this support can include the contraceptives themselves and surgical devices and drugs necessary for sterilizations and abortions. Beyond this, ODC help can include the equipment for field teams: jeeps, trucks, mobile operation vans, mobile motion picture theaters, loudspeaker systems, light aircraft, helicopters—whatever is required to bring the necessary technology to the target population and to persuade them to adopt it.

Most difficult to supply, of course, are the trained personnel to run the show. Many of these could be women, as indicated above, but in many nations social conditions and ideas of "appropriateness" would doubtless require men. Training centers should be established in the UDCs for organizing population control teams. In many countries these teams should be trained in public health, with population control as the major but not the sole function. The ODCs should be educating people right now for leadership in such training centers—and the medical profession should be showing the way.

We desperately need research in medical education

aimed at developing programs for training para-medical people to help with public health problems in both UDCs and ODCs. Unfortunately interest in such humanitarian goals seems to be the farthest thing from the minds of the A.M.A., an organization which cannot even come out forthrightly for abortion on demand in spite of the courageous efforts of many individual doctors. Clearly, one of the first jobs which must be undertaken in the United States is a thorough cleanup of its disgraceful health-care picture and a reorganization of the A.M.A. and the drug industry toward other than solely pecuniary goals. A great many American physicians are working earnestly for reform, and help from the public is long overdue.

Program Evaluation. Whatever efforts may be mounted in the UDCs, it is clear that unbiased evaluations of programs will have to be made continually. In our opinion, the best method of accomplishing this would be to establish a United Nations Bureau of the Census. U.N. teams would be given the job of overseeing census operations in all countries, rather than simply accepting the figures supplied by the nations themselves (as is now done). Uniform, dependable demographic data are essential to social scientists. The opening of borders to such teams could be a crucial first step towards partial surrender of sovereignty, a step which most people agree will have to come eventually if the crew of our spaceship is ever to live together in harmony. We hope that the United States would lead the way with a detailed proposal in this area, an offer of funds, and a unilateral opening of our borders to U.N. census teams with a guarantee of full cooperation from our Bureau of the Census. The avoidance of serious breaches of military security should not be difficult to work out.

Finally, let us make crystal clear our belief that population control aid flowing from ODCs to UDCs will only have a chance of success *once the ODCs have started to control their own populations and have ceased their exploitation of the UDCs.* Until that time, knowledgeable people in the UDCs will simply view any attempt to control their populations as one more imperialist-racist plot and will oppose it at every turn.

IV

The First-Class Cabins

THE PEOPLE WHO bear the primary responsibility for saving Spaceship Earth are the first-class passengers, those in the overdeveloped countries. They are the people who have contributed the most to the decline in safety of our craft, and they are the ones who have the resources to take corrective action. We have already discussed the need for reducing the numbers of people in the ODCs and some of the ways in which those nations might help UDCs to control their populations. In the next chapter, ways in which ODCs must aid UDCs to semi-develop will be considered. Here we will deal with the changes in behavior that must occur in the ODCs if they and our spacecraft are to remain intact, and we will discuss de-development, the process by which overdeveloped countries become developed countries.

De-development in the United States

Somewhere shortly after the Second World War the people of the United States made a colossal blunder. For a while after the war there was a lot of talk about joy, leisure, and a three day work week. People seemed to want a comfortable house, good food, an automobile for transportation, cold beer, and a chance to relax. Somehow all that went astray. TVs, boats, hi-fi's, driers, disposals, and a myriad other items appeared on the lists of "musts." Suddenly we needed two or three of everything, and a new model of each every year. And, consequently, many people were working 60 or more hours a week just to keep up the payments on an ever-mounting pile of junk. But, as the "affluence" of many of our citizens mounted, we somehow couldn't find the means to spread even a minimum of comfort to all our citizens. We accumulated, as Gunnar Myrdal [1] put it, an enormous "debt to the poor," a debt which "must be paid if the nation is not going to disintegrate or become a police state." (These two alternatives are not, of course, mutually exclusive!)

Our nation was taken over by an all-consuming lust for growth; growth as measured by a peculiar statistic, the gross national product (GNP). The GNP is a measure of a certain kind of economic growth—it is, in essence, the final value of the national annual output in goods and services. It most assuredly *is not* a measure of the standard of living or quality of life of the people. The social utility of a five million dollar bomber is equated with that of a five million dollar hospital. A sum of $20,000 paid for the services of an army general counts the same as $20,000 paid for the services of an architect. Increased profits in the health-care business due to increase in the level of emphysema (caused by air pollution) boosts the GNP. So do the profits of peddling DDT, cyclamates, cigarettes, and leaded gasoline.

Nowhere in the calculation of GNP are included factors measuring the cleanliness of the air, the death rate from hypertension, crime rates, the degree of personal freedom, of relaxation, and so on. During the decade of the 1960's, *while the GNP skyrocketed, the standard of living dropped.* And it is becoming increasingly obvious that without dramatic changes in our society in the fu-

---

[1] Myrdal, *The Challenge of World Poverty*, p. 383.

ture there will continue to be a negative correlation between the GNP and the *QOL* (Quality of Life).

What sorts of changes are needed? It is clear that Americans must rapidly reduce their negative impact on the life-support systems of the Earth, and they must dramatically reduce their wastage of the finite resources of the planet. They must also see to it that every American has adequate food, clothing, housing, medical care, and education. The de-development of the United States will be a big project indeed, but it can be accomplished to everyone's benefit if we have the will.

The "will" is the most important element. Americans must begin to question their fundamental assumptions. Is property really more valuable than human life? Does a person automatically have a high standard of living if he makes $50,000 per year and has two expensive cars, while his children are having their lives shortened by air pollution? Can a person have a high QOL if he or she is living under the threat of thermonuclear annihilation? Can a person have a high QOL while people are going hungry in his city? In his country? On his planet? Is it possible to be a humane, moral, happy human being in a nation which is waging war against a nation of poor peasants? Can one, indeed, be really happy with more than one's share? The cynical answer to the last question is a resounding "of course." But there is mounting evidence of deepseated unhappiness in our society—unhappiness so profound that only the muddle-headed would talk of a "Great Society" in the United States.

Part of the power to make a truly great society in the United States, and in the entire world, lies in the hands of today's very different young people. In our opinion, those who discount the magnitude of the present "generation gap," comparing it with generation gaps of the past, are fooling themselves. This is the first generation in history that has had such a wide opportunity to compare and contrast what their parents and schools *say* the society stands for, and what it actually *does* stand for. Television has been largely responsible for that, although post-World War II affluence and mobility have doubtless contributed also. This generation has seen changes in almost all areas of human endeavor which dwarf any experienced by those who matured before World War II. Man has entered a new era of rapid population growth, rapid consumption, rapid transportation, rapid communication, computerization, and suicidal weaponry. Man's capacity to *do,* and to *do fast,* has far outstripped his capacity for social adjustment.

The new era has been characterized by anthropologist Margaret Mead [2] as representing a new form of cultural evolution: prefiguration. She sees the development of a global culture based on today's youths who "have grown up in a world their elders never knew." The old "postfigurative culture" in which three or more generations live together and take for granted the same culture has largely disappeared. Its successor, "cofigurative culture," in which contemporaries serve as the prime cultural model, is also on the wane. Now culture, according to Dr. Mead, must become prefigurative—the new generation must lead the way, it must be the source of cultural innovation. "As I see it," she states,[3] "the development of prefigurational cultures will depend on the existence of a continuing dialogue in which the young, free to act on their own initiative, can lead their elders in the direction of the unknown. Then the older generation will have access to the new experiential knowledge, without which no meaningful plans can be made. It is only with the direct participation of the young, who have that knowledge, that we can build a viable future. . . . Out of their new knowledge—new to the world and new to us —must come the questions to those who are already equipped by education and experience to search for answers."

No thoughtful, informed person could dispute Dr.

[2] Margaret Mead, *Culture and Commitment: A Study of the Generation Gap* (Garden City, New York: Natural History Press/Doubleday, 1970).

[3] Mead, *Culture and Commitment,* p. 73.

Mead's evaluation of the scale and worldwide nature of the generation gap. Whether or not mankind will successfully make the transition to a prefigurative culture seems somewhat more doubtful—especially since most of the power to end the world rather than save it lies in the hands of those reared in earlier cultural forms. But then, the existence of a magnificent lady of Margaret Mead's maturity is enough to give one hope for humanity, and the behavior of many of our young people reenforces that hope.

A substantial segment of our youth is unwilling to accept the disparity between our slogans and our behavior, between the cornball rhetoric of our politicians and what our nation *does*. They are not primarily interested in the material accoutrements of our society, they are interested in themselves as human beings and in others as human beings. The standard arguments about how our young have been overprivileged, have never had to work for a living, and want to be parasitic on workers all contain some truth. It is also true that they, like many of their elders, often have half-baked ideas. The "Marxists" among them have often not read Marx and have seldom studied him. The "ecologists" among them are commonly ignorant of the laws of thermodynamics. None of this changes the situation one iota. Nor does pointing proudly to the anonymous millions of our youth who are marching mindlessly into the future, believing in the eternal verities of long-outdated comic books and studying baseball statistics.[4] The times they are a-changin', and it is difficult not to anticipate rapid change for the better as time swings the center of power towards those who are young today.

While we wait for that power shift, however, we must be pushing continually for other reforms. It is clear to us that a major step towards de-development of the

---

[4] Incredible as it may seem, the grandson of one President and son-in-law of another spent the first summer after Earth Day (April 22, 1970) in the nation's Capital as a baseball record statistician for the Washington Senators.

United States involves efforts to correct the inequities in our society, to heal the schisms as far as possible, and to find some national unity of purpose. Members of minority groups are not going to put their shoulders to the wheel to help save a white racist society which will offer them no fair share of the fruits of success, should we pull through the current crisis. Hardhats and long-hairs are not going to work together toward common goals unless those common goals seem real to both groups. Is there some possibility of finding such goals?

We think there is, and we think that with some national leadership they can be found. For instance, many of the tensions between blue collar whites and blacks have economic roots. The Indochina war has absorbed vast resources which could have been put into improving the economic lot of our minority peoples. The same war has caused an inflation which threatens the security of lower middle-class whites. The "middle Americans" have long been told that if they worked hard, were patriotic and obeyed the laws, they would have the finest rewards American society could offer: two cars, TV, steak, and beer. They worked hard, were patriotic and obeyed the law, but found themselves up to their ears in debt and eating day-old bread. Small wonder they are unhappy seeing their tax dollars go to set up job-training programs for blacks. They see themselves in deep trouble and simultaneously feel they are expected to finance their own economic competition.

The blacks on the other hand are now exercising power to improve their economic condition. They quite naturally have little sympathy for their white oppressors, regardless of the economic status of the whites. They want their piece of the action; they have been too long delayed in getting it.

Antagonistic as these two groups are, both clearly have the same goals: to be able to work in peace toward reasonable economic goals, and to have a substantial amount of leisure time to be able to do their own thing. Even in a de-developed United States, both groups should be able to reach these goals without severe competition. But two principal things will have to change before that can happen. First, the nation must stop squandering its resources on efforts like the Indochina war, the huge military establishment we presently support, and the space program. And second, we must convert from a "cowboy economy" to a "spaceman economy," with a major feature of the conversion being a dramatic change in our idea of "needs."

It is only a slight exaggeration to think of the advertising industry as an industry whose primary goal is to create irrational "needs." Its secondary goal is to suppress competition based on quality by creating illusory differences between identical products. The whole purpose of creating these "needs" is to generate sales and promote economic growth, which might seem fine and dandy except that the sort of economic growth promoted by most advertising is precisely what must be stopped. At the behest of the various corporate constellations, with which it has mutually dependent relationships, the advertising industry has persuaded Americans that automobiles are ego-building sex symbols rather than devices for transportation. With the blessing of the FDA, advertising has called American white bread "enriched," when almost all the nutrients are removed and then a few of the cheapest replaced (recent experiments show that rats fed exclusively on such bread starve to death). Advertising has created the "need" for myriad power gimmicks, and promoted fancy, deceptive and disposable packaging. Advertising has given the word "old" a perjorative meaning and has helped to find ways to make things "old" before their time. During the 1960's, advertising with the backing of business, labor and government, spearheaded what Professor D. I. Bilderback has called "a conspiracy against frugality." During the past decade or so, people were encouraged to spend, to borrow and to spend some more, with the borrowing often to be done at 18 per cent true annual interest rates or more. The idea that one might have enough worldly goods to be satisfied was never heard, and even appeals for depositers in banks and savings and loans companies often emphasized saving for future purchases of consumer goods. In doing all this, advertising has merely been "doing its job"—but effectively enough to bring us to the verge of disaster.

As a side effect advertising has also created an aura of broad-based affluence; an aura which has helped conceal the depths of poverty occupied by a substantial proportion of Americans, and has even more effectively helped to conceal the existence of a true ruling class in American society by pushing amusing ideas such as "people's capitalism." "People's capitalism" is supposed to exist because so many people own stock in American businesses. It is true that at the beginning of 1969 more than 26,000,000 Americans were shareholders, but the amount of stock owned by the vast majority of these is trivial, and the power that stock represents, nil.[5] Indeed so much of the power and prosperity in the United States is actually vested in a few hands that it resembles, in that respect, underdeveloped Latin American countries more than it resembles such Western European nations as England and France. Ferdinand Lundberg described the United States, aside from its industrial features, as a "Banana Republic *par excellence*[6]. A major step in de-development, then, must be to clamp severe controls on the media, especially on advertising in the media. Such suggestions will, of course, immediately raise a cry of fascism and restriction of freedom of speech. However, the reverse would be true; freedom of speech could be extended while freedom to misrepresent is restricted. The FCC could see to it that news programing was expanded and made more free

---

[5] See the discussion of "people's capitalism" on pp. 12-13 in Ferdinand Lundberg's *The Rich and the Super-Rich* (New York: Bantam Books, 1968). This book has a detailed and heavily documented discussion of the distribution of wealth in the United States.

[6] Lundberg, p. 6.

both from economic and from bureaucratic pressures. Control over advertising could be done through legislation in three ways. First of all, truth-in-advertising laws with real teeth could be passed with fines large enough to threaten a business with bankruptcy and stiff jail terms for corporate criminals found guilty by a jury. Secondly, substantial free time should be donated to the Consumer's Union (or its equivalent) for comparative product reports—each designed to be the length of a standard commercial.

The third and ultimate control on advertising would be exercised by control of what products might or might not be manufactured and offered for sale. Hopefully, when Americans wake up to their peril, a governmental reorganization will be one of the first reforms instituted. Such a reorganization might include a single Department of Population and Environment (*DPE*), given broad powers to maintain the QOL. One of the major roles of a Department of Population and Environment would be to determine, with the help of ad hoc review panels, the social value and environment-resource threat of each class of products. It could then, subject to an appeals procedure, ban or restrict the production of the product. Intensive study would plainly be necessary to minimize DPE blunders in this area, and we would not presume to have the expertise to advocate specific decisions. Here, however, are some of the kinds of decisions the DPE might take. Consider a possible future directive from the Department.

"DPE Directive XII. Summary. *Private Automobiles*. Private automobiles are for transportation only, and all advertisements concerning them shall deal only with the transportation virtues of the vehicle. No private automobile shall have an empty weight of over 2400 pounds, nor shall it have an internal combustion engine developing more than 100 horsepower or with a compression ratio exceeding 6:1. Engine design, emission control and safety standards are detailed in DPE TechDoc SA-301, recycling standards in DPE TechDoc RA-301. Unless waived under form DPE-W6, or DPE-W7, no family unit shall own more than one private automobile at a time."

Pretty harassing? Not necessarily. Cars *are* for transportation, and proper use of the media could once again persuade American men to get their sexual kicks out of sex (not reproduction) instead of a series of automotive sexual surrogates. Restriction of families to ownership of single small cars also would put sôme pressure against over-reproducers. Our stress on the world's supply of nonrenewable resources would be greatly alleviated by limiting the fuel consumption of the cars and by designing them for recycling. For instance, simply by substituting aluminum for copper in construction of automobiles, the quality of scrap can be improved to the point where it is cheaper to use scrap to make new cars than to refine more steel from iron ore. Cars could mandatorily be designed and built for recycling and guaranteed for 200,000 miles or 20 years (whichever came first). It should be a serious federal offense to abandon an automobile—required recycling would help to remove a major scenic blight from our landscape. A refundable 10 per cent deposit on each car would make it worthwhile for car owners to turn in old vehicles.

Of course the most immediate reward of restricting the size and number of automobiles and controlling the design of their engines would be environmental. Automobiles in the United States are estimated to be responsible for as much as 80 per cent of urban air pollution and perhaps 40 per cent of air pollution nationwide, although they account for less than 20 per cent of our power consumption. Smaller cars could greatly cut the exhaust component of air pollution, especially if lead-free gasoline were mandatory. (We would of course need other smog control devices as well.) Smaller tires would reduce the amount of air pollution caused by vaporization of tires, and that component could be made less hazardous by banning certain substances (such as the polychlorinated biphenols, environmentally dangerous relatives of DDT) from use by tire manufacturers.

Other potential benefits from an auto-control program are legion. Cars would be more efficient transportation—better traffic flow and movement would be possible because roads would be less crowded, parking would be easier (bigs cars take up a lot of space). As soon as a concerted campaign to remove the old "boats" from the road had been completed, driving would be safer, since the smaller cars would be easier to handle and engineered for safety and durability. Monthly payments would be smaller too.

But, you say, many people want or need special purpose vehicles such as station wagons or pick-ups with campers. Hopefully, as the "American way of life" changed to one oriented toward fewer possessions and less machinery, this demand would slacken. More and more public land could be converted into wilderness areas in which motorized camping was banned; people could be encouraged to regain an appreciation of their place in nature.

But even such a trend would leave many legitimate uses for special purpose vehicles, including, of course, camping for those physically unable to back-pack. Business vehicles could be purchased under a permit system, their design durability and safety being controlled in a manner similar to that of private cars. A system of government licensed (and perhaps partially subsidized) agencies for leasing special-purpose vehicles could be set up to provide for whatever level of usage is determined to be ecologically acceptable.

Over the longer term, America's transportation system could be redesigned to minimize the need for automobiles and trucks and maximize the use of feet and bicycles for local transport and trains and aircraft, i.e. public transport, for long distances. Cities could be redesigned so that people would be able to live near their work. With street pollution controls placed on industry, this could be both pleasant and convenient. Television-phone ordering and efficient delivery systems could minimize the need for driving in connection with shopping. Indeed such improved communications (relatively cheap in terms of both resource and power consumption compared to the requirements of the present alternatives) could operate from desks in citizens' own homes. An added bonus is that more exercise from walking and bicycling, less frustrating commuting, and a less frantic life would combine with reduced smog levels to produce a much healthier population.

Other possible DPE decisions in connection with the de-development of the U.S.A. may be rather easily imagined. For instance, detergents may be banned from home use (they already have been in Suffolk County, New York). In spite of the ludicrous ads on television, few, if any, American women are stupid enough to spend time competing with their neighbors over whose wash is whiter. Soap or nonpolluting detergents will be quite sufficient for cleanliness in most circumstances, and much more preferable ecologically. Softened water would make the use of soap practical where it is not now. Water softening can be done quite economically at the municipal level.

The DPE will need to determine durability and recycling requirements for major appliances as well as for automobiles. In some cases, such as refrigerators, the basic mechanisms are already exceedingly durable. It is primarily the frills—plastic liners, butter warmers, ice cube makers, and so on—which break down. Once people accept the role of the refrigerator as a device for cooling food, each family will be able to own one such device per generation or so. Indeed, laws may well be passed strictly limiting the number of appliances a single family may possess. Learning to survive with only one TV set will, for instance, be simpler than learning to live on a planet made uninhabitable by an unending quest for material possessions.

Undoubtedly, there would be many other restrictions. Power lawnmowers would become extinct in suburbia as, in many areas, would lawns. People in those areas might learn to plant attractive arrays of native plants rather than struggling with pesticides, fertilizers, and mowers to keep a monoculture of grass under control. And as a result their lives, and those of their neighbors, will become quieter, more relaxed, and less polluted.

It goes without saying that the DPE would clamp down on all governmental and industrial polluters. The most basic laws of physics tell us it is always easier to contain pollutants at their source than to clean them from the environment once they have been released. It is cheaper, too, for society as a whole. When a polluter is allowed to dump noxious substances into air or water, he is also allowed to pass on part of his costs of doing business to us. We pay when we repurify our water in order to drink it. We pay when we have to paint our smog-assaulted homes more frequently. We pay the doctor bills as smog-induced emphysema kills more of us. Since due to those same laws of physics, *some* pollution is inevitable, the DPE will have to devise a system of pollution taxes so that the public may be reimbursed for industrial use of public air and water. In the language of accounting, businessmen must be forced to internalize their externalities.

It is especially critical that a DPE or similar agency set and enforce *national* pollution abatement standards. Otherwise states with high standards will put their businesses at a disadvantage relative to those in states with low standards. Moreover, pollutants, from DDT to raw sewage, are not respecters of state lines.

Perhaps the most difficult job of the DPE will be the regulation of pollution produced by state and local governments. We are confident, however, that a clever mix of federal aid, federal fines, and, where appropriate, jail sentences can be devised to do the job. After all, why should not the widespread dissemination of poison be considered a criminal act? Surely, after national defense, the first duty of the United States government is to prevent the slow destruction of the United States through environmental deterioration. The task is enormous and the enemies many—including such rapacious groups in the private sector as real-estate developers and ambitious juggernauts within the federal government such as the Army Corps of Engineers. *Ways must be found to control all of them.*

Consider for a moment one of the prime activities that results in environmental deterioration: the generation and use of electric power. Europeans live a pleasant, reasonably affluent life on somewhat less than one-half the per capita electric power consumption of Americans, and with careful planning their level of consumption could also be greatly reduced. Amazingly, though, the American power industry wants to *increase* our per capita consumption at a rate that will double our national use of power every decade. At this rate, every square inch of the United States would be covered with conventional power plants in two hundred years or so.

This projected increase is the reason that the industry is vigorously promoting the construction of more heavily-subsidized nuclear powerplants, perhaps the most dangerous single trend in the environment-technology area today. They are urged on by the agency which has the tasks both of promoting and regulating the use of atomic energy—the Atomic Energy Commission (AEC). The AEC has a long record of ecological and biological incompetence. Two of the country's top health physicists, employed at the AEC-supported Lawrence Radiation Laboratory, have attacked the basis of the AEC standards for permissible emission of radioactive substances from power plants. Dr. John W. Gofman and Dr. Arthur R. Tamplin have presented impressive evidence that the guidelines for radiation exposure of the population-at-large are set at least *ten times too high*. The emotional reaction of the AEC to this disclosure will come as no surprise to those familiar with the AEC's role in past environmental controversies, ranging all the way back to the long and fortunately successful battle of biologists to halt above-ground nuclear testing.

Fundamentally, an agency of repeatedly proven incompetence is all that stands between us and the virtually permanent poisoning of the entire environment of our spaceship by the widespread and premature use of fission reactor technology. Whether power generation by fission can eventually be both safe and economical is problematical, but *there is no question that it cannot be either today*. There is one point on which all competent scientists agree: the AEC must be dismembered so that the promotion and regulation of the uses of atomic energy no longer rest in the same hands.

But, in spite of the chance of making Spaceship Earth uninhabitable, our power industry forges bravely ahead, willing to take whatever risk, because, as John A. Carver, Jr. of the Federal Power Commission said recently, Americans will be in "a race for their lives" to meet electric power needs over the next thirty years. Strangely, those poor Europeans with less than one half of our power don't seem to be in such a race, but this fine point is not grasped by the keen minds of those who run our power companies. No, rather than taking the only possible intelligent step to solve our power dilemma, they are hard at work *trying to increase the demand that they predict we will be in a life-and-death race to meet*! You know the ploy—open your electric bill and out drops a pretty brochure or card (printed at your expense) urging you to buy yet another power-hungry appliance.

The obvious course out of the problems created by our power glut is *to find ways to lower the demand for power*. Except in special circumstances, all construction of power generating facilities should cease immediately, and power companies should be forbidden to encourage people to use more power. *Power is much too cheap*. It should certainly be made more expensive and perhaps rationed, in order to reduce its frivolous use.

Plans should be made immediately and programs initiated to move society to a less power-hungry way of life. The aluminum industry, for instance, is an enormous consumer of electricity, and a substantial portion of that power is used to make aluminum beer cans. It is our contention that society can function beautifully with a *gain* in the QOL if beer is consumed from returnable glass bottles, rather than from aluminum cans. Deposits on the bottles could be made large enough so that virtually all would be returned, helping to add to the esthetic QOL or at least to the esthetic quality of the lives of those who prefer an unlittered environment. Safety on beaches would be improved as the chances of stepping on discarded razor-sharp pull tabs is diminished. And, of course, environmental quality in general would improve as power consumption is reduced, since fewer polluting power plants would be required.

An alternative strategy would be to keep making aluminum beer cans (and other cans, too), make the tabs non-removable, and put a high deposit (say 25¢) on the return of the cans. With such a premium, those cans thrown into the countryside would be collected and returned by children. Whether or not this would be an ecologically sound strategy would depend on calculations of the amount of energy required to recycle beer cans and the amount of energy required to transport, clean, and relabel the heavier and bulkier bottles. We do not propose to do such calculations here, but this is an example of the kind of reckoning society must quickly learn to do and act upon.

Other possible ways to conserve power are myriad. Who, for instance, benefits from the garish use of electric signs that deface the nighttime sky of our cities? Many of them, of course, carry the kind of deceptive advertising that fuels our frenzied economy. Shutting them down will save power on the spot and will also save power by removing the "need" to manufacture a lot of junk. Advertising signs on restaurants, motels, and the like could be shut off by law at night when the establishment was not open. If everyone had to do it there would be little, if any, competitive loss.

Air conditioning is another great power drain which could in large part be closed. It should immediately be made illegal to construct a building with windows which cannot be opened. Certainly, air conditioning is important where people must work around hot machines, or where a controlled environment is necessary for such things as assembling delicate electronic gadgets. But the summer heat can be beaten by most of us in many other ways (as it had to be beaten by all of us only two or three decades ago!) If we succeed in changing our way of life, long summer vacations can be part of the new, relaxed mode. In redesigned cities, clean air, green parks, and municipal swimming pools will help make life pleasant. Air and water-filtration units would become unnecessary. We could move toward more sensible modes of dress—shorts and short-sleeved shirts can become acceptable summer business wear for men.

What will we do with all the unemployed air conditioner repair men, employees of automobile manufacturers, aluminum workers, and the like? That is where the planning comes in. The work force will, over a period of time, be greatly reduced in two ways. First of all, with population control the total number of people will eventually be reduced and the work force with it. Secondly, we should set a target of a maximum work week of 20 hours, which, since most people now work 40 hours or more, would amount to more than doubling the number of jobs. As we get more and more efficient at producing our desired per capita "product," the average work week might even be reduced much below that.

During the transition decades, there will be plenty for displaced workers to do. The automobile industry, for instance, will develop a great deal of spare productive capacity as the size and turnover rate of cars drops. Ways can be found to turn that capacity to socially desirable goals and then phase it out as the process of de-development proceeds. Temporarily it could be turned to answering two massive real needs of our society; the need for new housing for the substantial portion of our population that now lives in urban ghettos or rural slums and the need for mass transit systems for our cities.

While we divest ourselves of surplus junk we can use part of our excess capacity to extend both necessities and amenities to those now without them.

Much of the productive capacity of our society, once we decide to go off the junk standard, could be used to improve the quality of life of Americans. As we shall see in the next chapter, a great deal of that capacity could also be employed to improve the QOL of our fellow passengers now traveling in steerage. Over a period of several decades, American industrial power (as well as that of the other ODCs) could be used in a great campaign to renovate Spaceship Earth. Then that power can be reduced to the level necessary for a sophisticated campaign of preventive maintenance.

During the renovation period, work would go on continually to see to it that the human capital of the ODCs is fully prepared for what will follow. The mass media will help the average person to escape the thrall of the "Protestant ethic"—the pernicious idea that hard work and suffering are somehow, *per se,* desirable. Large numbers of people will be able to return to school, increase their intellectual resources, and thus be able to face the prospect of increased leisure with equanimity. Eventually expanded adult education programs would help provide employment for teachers displaced by reduced numbers of youngsters entering school. At present, in fact, our schools are so miserably understaffed and there are so many children not getting a full or proper education that it would be some time before teachers could expect relief from their overcrowded classes.

In general, we should be moving more and more of our economic activities out of the sphere of producing goods and into the sphere of providing services. With more effort going into the service side of the economy, the quality of these services could be greatly improved. One obvious target would be our now disgraceful health services, with their desperate need for more highly trained and dedicated physicians, nurses, and public health workers. Recent events have highlighted the low quality of most American law enforcement agencies. Much more education and training, as well as education of the general public, will be needed to elevate the police to the role of highly respected professionals which they should occupy in society. While the need for brute police force will decrease as we move from a cowboy to a spaceman economy, the need for intelligent officers well grounded in the law, psychology, and so on will increase. Much the same can be said about the men who control our run-down penal system which itself needs complete restructuring; the judges who try to keep our creaky, overloaded courts functioning would clearly welcome a more intelligent approach to crime fully as much as the reduced crime rate that would inevitably develop. In three professional areas, *at least,* teaching, medicine, and the law, there will not be any need for a reduction in the work force.

A new day will dawn for the repair man. In a society which does not encourage the discarding of all malfunctioning items, skilled repair will once again be highly prized. So will good cooking, gardening, and the hand-making of fine furniture, pottery, and the like. Fine workmanship will regain its value. Artists and actors will no longer have to "struggle," as their nonmaterial assets once again are valued by society as a whole. Many more people will have time to become politically active, politicians will enjoy a more respected position in society, and control of the United States can truly come to rest in the hands of an informed electorate.

Social Justice in the United States

Can such a utopian situation really develop in our country? Not, we think, without making some dramatic changes in the way we treat our citizens. *All* Americans must be recruited into the de-development program; all must be assured of sharing the fruits of success. Those who have been effectively excluded from our society will surely block our attempts to save it—unless the doors are opened to them. What is needed is obvious; how to get it less so. In spite of two decades of "progress," nonwhite Americans remain second- and third-class citizens in a white racist country. Twenty years is too long to wait, but in 1976 these citizens will have been waiting for two hundred years. It is now often stated by the members of our ruling aristocracy that there are limits beyond which making laws about equal treatment and opportunity have no effect. You know the speech—it usually ends with a pious sentence about the need for changing "the hearts and minds of Americans." Yet it is apparently beyond their capacity to teach many in our midst a few simple biological facts. They cannot (or will not), for instance, persuade a substantial part of our population that a black skin and the person inside it are intrinsically as good as a white skin and the person inside of it. A cynical person might be moved to consider that various kinds of personal gain are involved in the "southern strategies" that permeate white society—votes for politicians, money for exploiters, and the ego boost of feeling "superior" for those with little else available to inflate their self-esteem.

Whatever the reasons for the continuance of racism in this country, it is apparent that a courageous government could take momentous strides toward its rapid termination both by insisting on more positive approaches to this problem through the communications media, and by the strictest and swiftest possible enforcement of civil rights legislation. A massive program for housing, job training and re-education would go a long way toward convincing die-hard racists that theirs is a lost cause.

Abraham Lincoln said in 1858 that the United States could not "endure permanently half slave and half free." More than 100 years later the division between first and second class citizens again threatens our national survival; a racially polarized nation will be incapable of coping with the population-environment crisis. In the words of the *Report of the National Advisory Commission on Civil Disorders* (Kerner Report):

"What white Americans have never fully understood —but what the Negro can never forget—is that white society is deeply implicated in the ghetto. White institutions created it, white institutions maintain it, and white society condones it.

"It is time now to turn with all the purpose at our command to the major unfinished business of this nation. It is time to adopt strategies for action that will produce quick and visible progress. It is time to make good the promises of American democracy to all citizens —urban and rural, white and black, Spanish-surname, American Indian, and every minority group."

Those words were written in 1968. There is no sign that our government or most of our white citizens are acting on them. If we want our nation to survive, we had better get with it.

De-Development in the other ODCs

A brief word must be added here about the de-development of Canada, Australia, Japan, Western Europe, the Soviet Union and the other ODCs. In most of those with corporate states more or less resembling the United States, many of the problems will be similar to those already discussed for the United States. All of those countries will have the advantage of lower *per capita* power consumption at the outset, but many (especially in Western Europe) have the disadvantage of already being even more grossly overpopulated in other ways than the United States.

The major Communist ODC, the Soviet Union, also has not achieved the extreme state of overdevelopment of the United States, but it is striving toward it. It has the additional advantage of having within its borders a much higher proportion of the resources it needs than does the United States. The Soviet Union appears to be slowly awakening to environmental problems. Pollution of rivers has seriously reduced sturgeon populations, cutting into supplies of highly prized caviar. A standard joke in Soviet scientific circles these days is that the magnificent Russian technology has saved the day by creating an artificial caviar which is absolutely indistinguishable from the real thing—except by taste!

But the Soviet government, like the government of almost all other ODCs, is far behind ours in recognizing the seriousness of the population-resource-environment crisis. One would hope that, once it was recognized, their great centralization of power would permit them to take corrective measures much more rapidly than is presently possible in the United States.

At the moment there is little that Americans can do to encourage de-development of the other ODCs, except to work for the de-development of the United States. The United States could set the pace for the world both in cleaning up its internal mess and in shifting from a program of raping the UDCs to one of helping them. We can hope that the other ODCs will quickly follow our example, especially if they are urged along by clever propaganda and appropriate changes in America's economic and political relations with them. If they do not go along, everyone will pay the consequences.

It may be presumptuous to assume that if we do not take a sensible course, no one else will. But logic and necessity require that we put our own house in order before we can even begin to help or guide others. It is true that our survival does indeed depend on world survival *but*—make no mistake—nobody else is going to plan our survival for us.

The effort must start with us, right here. That is the step that precedes all others.

V

Steerage

"BASICALLY THERE ARE not many oases left in a vast, almost world-wide network of slums; about 450 million well-fed people living in comparative luxury . . . as against 2,400 million undernourished, malnourished, or in other ways deficiently fed and generally poor. . . ." Thus food scientist Georg Borgstrom described in 1969 the imbalance between the small numbers of people traveling first class on Spaceship Earth, and the masses in steerage. Most of the steerage passengers, of course, live in UDCs, countries which today carry about 70 per cent of the world's population, and which in the year 2000 are projected to contain well over 80 per cent. Unless something extraordinary happens, the poor and the miserable will make up an even larger percentage of the Earth's population in the year 2000 than they do today. Since the entire population will then be almost twice as large, the absolute number of people living in misery probably will be more than doubled.

This unhappy course can only be altered in two ways. Disaster may intervene, raising the death rate, reducing the population, and perhaps catapulting most or all of the first-class passengers into steerage. Or, a concerted world effort, heavily backed by the ODCs, many manage both to slow population growth and to improve the lot of the majority of the world's poor.

Semi-Development

It is perfectly clear that development of the UDCs into industrialized countries modeled on today's ODCs is impossible.[1] The phenomenal amounts of raw materials required to do the job may not exist at all, and the environment could not endure the trauma of their extraction and use if they do. Too many people have automatically assumed that there is a continuum from underdevelopment to development along which developing nations might proceed. Implicit in the terminology was the notion that development was "good," underdevelopment "bad." This simplistic view is no longer useful. Fortunately, the combination of physical and attitudinal changes that produced the development of the United States, the USSR, Europe, Japan and a few other areas can never be repeated. The idea that they represent some sort of ultimate good is simply an example of Western cultural chauvinism, an idea we have sold not only to ourselves but also to people in the UDCs. In order to help break this pattern of thought, two terms were coined: "over-development," to indicate that classical development can go much too far, and "semi-development," to indicate that total industrialization of the entire world is not required to provide everyone with a satisfying life. With a less industrialized, less GNP-oriented, less frontier-style existence in today's ODCs and a more industrialized, healthier, less laissez-faire existence in today's UDCs, a cooperative world should be able to obtain a reasonably decent quality of life for all.

There is a problem with the term "semi-development." It has too much of the connotation of a way-

---

[1] We are painfully aware that throughout the following section we advocate proposals which may seem to contravene the Third World aspirations to absolute economic self-determination. Unfortunately, the state of the world is now such that neither ODCs nor UDCs can any longer afford such luxuries.

station on the road to better things. The changes that are needed in the UDCs are only partially along the road taken by the ODCs; "development" in the old sense is not what everyone should want and certainly not what they should have. It is not the only way to obtain the biological necessities for everyone (in fact it has not resulted in the supplying of those necessities to all the citizens of the ODCs), and it seems now to be eroding amenities faster than it can provide substitutes. Many UDCs would do well to emulate Cuba and give strong priority to agriculture rather than industry in the development of their economies. Castro has moved in the right direction, although political factors and his own inclinations have contributed to a serious overdependence on a sugar monoculture. Cuba is now reportedly beginning to emphasize agricultural diversification.[2] If one assumes, as we do, that the QOL is intimately related to the number of options open to each individual, it can be argued that development will always lead ultimately to a lowered QOL; that the restrictions imposed by industrialization will always eventually counterbalance the freedoms opened up. Clearly, though, society must restrict certain options, such as extreme materialism, in order to maximize the number which remain open.

A way must be found for UDCs to shape their own cultural destinies, as free as possible from interference from the overbearing nations of the West. However, at the same time, the UDCs must become capable of supplying their citizens with the biological necessities of life and, beyond that, the amenities for a satisfying existence. In order to do that fundamental changes must take place in the UDCs. These changes will, in part, move the UDCs in directions taken earlier by the ODCs in the process of their development. But this will only be a partial move, although in the same *general* direction.

In most cases this semi-development will consist of

[2] Lee Lockwood. *Castro's Cuba, Cuba's Fidel* (New York: Random House, Vintage ed., 1967).

programs designed to produce agricultural self-sufficiency, not industrial self-sufficiency or even extensive industrialization. The cultural course chosen by UDCs will unquestionably involve the acquisition of manufactured items—bicycles, refrigerators, electric lights, etc. —by many of their citizens. *But this does not mean that each UDC must develop the capacity to manufacture all these items.* Most manufactured goods should be obtained from countries already industrialized—from the ODCs. In order for a sufficient flow of such goods to move toward the UDCs, carefully planned but drastic changes will have to be made in the world trade system.

The trading role of the UDCs was established largely during colonial times, and has since been deteriorating steadily. The UDCs are mostly suppliers of primary commodities—rubber, coffee, tea, cocoa, tin, and cheap hand-crafted products. Such goods account for a decreasing share of world trade, both because of an increasing volume in manufactured goods and because technology has permitted ODCs to substitute their own manufactured products for primary commodities (e.g. synthetic rubber for natural rubber, synthetic fibers for natural fibers). Ironically, the manufacture and use of these synthetics cause some of the most severe environmental problems in the ODCs!

The industries of the UDCs face formidable difficulties whenever they attempt to compete with ODC industries in international trade. It is usually difficult even for ODC industries to move into new foreign markets already well served by others. Not only do UDC industries often lack the management know-how and skilled labor available in ODCs, they also suffer because of their own self-imposed import restrictions, applied under the pretense of ameliorating their foreign exchange problems, but in practice allowing inefficient manufacturers to produce inferior goods for the domestic markets. These inferior goods cannot compete on the international market; if they could they would truly ameliorate the foreign exchange situation. The pitfalls of protectivism are, of course, an old story to economists and historians. The UDCs' position is further weakened by high import duties often imposed by ODCs on commodities and on semi-finished and manufactured goods. These tariff barriers often make it impossible for UDC industries to participate in foreign markets.

If this situation is permitted to go on, the trading prospects of the UDCs will simply continue to deteriorate. But it cannot be permitted to continue. Just as no properly run nation would permit a geographical area within the country to be forced deeper and deeper into poverty because of the internal trade situation, similarly no sane world would permit a bloc of nations containing the majority of human beings to drift in the same direction because of malfunctioning of the international trade situation.[3]

Clearly ODCs must adjust their tariffs so that imports from UDCs, particularly of finished goods, are encouraged. Beyond that an even more fundamental change in attitude is required. By today's standards, world trade may have to remain permanently unbalanced. That is, the flow of goods from ODCs to UDCs will remain more valuable than the flow from UDCs to ODCs. Just as within the United States not all parts of the country are required to contribute equally to its material welfare, so not all countries of the world should contribute an equal per capita share of its industrial production.

---

[3] It is, however, possible to argue that the basic disparity is between a worldwide industrial complex and nonindustrial areas. Often, even within countries, areas which supply commodities are exploited by industrial areas. In France the peasants were so systematically looted for the benefit of the industrial workers that DeGaulle had to face a peasant revolt. The Canadian South is now engaged in a major struggle over who shall have the right to exploit the North; and the people of the North, native and European, will have little say in what happens to them. One could also argue that Texas has received less benefit from its oil than has Arabia, and it is apparent that the Arctic coast of Alaska is about to be raped for the good of the American oil industry.

What is needed is a change in our accounting procedures so that physical and biological realities are entered into the books before they are balanced. We must add to the usual economic ideas of value, as established by supply, demand, and marginal utility, some measures of ecological costs (related to the "total utility"' of the economist). For instance, the air, water, and microbial waste disposal systems of this planet have very low marginal utilities. This means that they are abundant and the cost of getting the use of more per individual is low. Their total utility is high, to say the least. Without them, we cannot survive. Now, an economist might say, "never fear, if our supplies of clean air, fresh water, or waste disposal capacity are threatened, their marginal utility will rise, and then it will pay someone to restore or clean up the supplies." When the cost of getting more goes up, someone will go to work to make money by providing more.

This may make good economic sense, but it is lousy physics and biology. It is all too easy to cross a water pollution threshold, suddenly rendering a previously abundant water supply virtually useless for many purposes. The costs of refurbishing it may then become financially astronomical and ecologically unacceptable (as an example of the latter, extraordinarily expensive and dangerous nuclear desalting plants are often proposed as a way around the progressive salting up of the world's fresh water supplies). Similarly, if enough pollution is injected into the atmosphere, irreversible and disastrous climatic changes may be entrained, and nature's waste disposal systems may be irreversibly poisoned by synthetic chemicals released into the environment.

The value, then, of our life-support systems cannot be judged in standard economic terms. The buffering capacity of the planetary environment cannot be treated simply as a commodity with a large marginal utility, because the more of it we use, the greater the threat of *decreasing* its total utility! It is largely the ODCs which are threatening this total utility by placing disproportionate strains on our life-support systems. Together with the virtual impossibility of obtaining the resources of industrialization of the UDCs (even if the ODCs should dramatically limit their usage), this means that a differential in industrialization and associated environmental impact will exist between today's ODCs and UDCs, even after they have changed into developed and semi-developed nations respectively. This differential will probably be permanent and will certainly persist until the planetary population is reduced far below its present size.

Therefore, UDCs will be foregoing much-desired industrialization in order to keep the planet habitable, a sacrifice much to the benefit of the ODCs also. The ODCs should be willing to be taxed to pay for this service performed by the UDCs for the life-support systems. This tax could take the form of changes in the international trade system so that it strongly *favored* UDCs, rather than discriminating against them as the present system does. The system should be monitored by an international body in such a way that the UDCs are guaranteed a flow of the manufactured goods and industrial services which are required for whatever form of the good life each nation seeks to attain (within ecologically determined limits, of course).

Growing More Food

The central problem of most UDCs is agricultural development. Food production must be enormously increased in the next few decades if we are to continue to feed the growing numbers of people, even at the present miserable dietary level. Recent success with high-yield "miracle" grains has created the impression in some circles that the distribution of the seeds of such grains will solve the food problem in the UDCs. We are on the verge of a Green Revolution, they say.

The idea behind this Green Revolution is fundamentally sound. Yields will be increased on land already under cultivation, using new strains of crops traditionally grown. This approach avoids the serious problems of bringing additional land under cultivation. The latter process may be extremely expensive, requiring clearing, terracing, removal of rocks, the breaking up of hard pan, the installation of irrigation systems or some combination of these. Other costs of opening new land include those of resettling people, building homes, schools, hospitals, etc. and the cost of administration. In seven UDC projects, per acre costs of opening new land ranged from $32 to $873, with the median cost at $218. Usually the costs would be even higher, since much of the potentially arable land of the UDCs would require irrigation, which alone now costs almost $400 per acre.

The ecological costs of opening new land are also high. Forest land is stripped, reducing the water-retaining capacity of watersheds. Local climate is changed, as is the amount of sunlight reflected by the area, thus contributing to the alteration of the entire Earth's climate. Furthermore, complex ecological communities are replaced by crop monocultures, a process which reduces the overall stability of the ecological systems of the planet.

An additional advantage to the increased-yield approach is that farmers do not have to learn to grow entirely different kinds of crops, and consumers do not have to adjust to entirely new foods. Agriculture tends to be one of man's most conservative activities, and although traditional patterns can be broken under the proper circumstances, minimizing the required changes is obviously important. Likewise, those people who are hungriest are unfortunately often those who are most conservative in their eating habits. Accustomed to a very limited diet, they do not take readily to novel foods.

Given that the fundamental idea of the Green Revolution is a sound one, what needs to be done to maximize its success? First of all, it is important to recognize that much more than the distribution of new high-yielding grain seeds is required. High-yield strains do not achieve their potential unless given adequate fertilizer (they are fertilizer-sensitive), plenty of water, and proper cultivation. Fertilizer must be obtained by the nation and supplied to the farmer, either through purchases overseas or the building of fertilizer plants. Both require capital. The construction of roads and the purchase of vehicles on which fertilizer can be moved to farms (and on which produce can be moved to market) also requires capital. So does the drilling of wells, the building of irrigation systems and the purchase of pesticides.

Money, then, is needed for the Green Revolution to work. And it is not only money for farm inputs. There must also be a suitable market for the produce once it is grown; there must be money available for the purchase of food. Hungry people are usually destitute and do not create a demand for food in the marketplace. The marketplace responds only to money. That is why agricultural economists make the seemingly paradoxical statement that one way to fight starvation is "to increase the demand for food." If progressive farmers produce large crops but the demand (in money) is not sufficient, prices will fall and the incentive for the farmer to continue high-cost inputs and hard labor will be reduced or destroyed.

Another desperate need in UDC agriculture is for trained technicians. For instance, while the Netherlands in 1960 had 133 agricultural research workers for each 100,000 people active in agriculture and Japan had 60, Colombia had only 9, Pakistan 4.5, and India 1.2. Such people are essential if farmers are to learn how to achieve maximum results with new strains. There are also serious problems in the ingrained attitudes of UDC farmers. Many, in places like India, do not share the ambitions of most ODC farmers, and have limited goals of economic improvement. How thoroughly and how fast this crust of tradition can be broken remains an open question. As Bernard Nossiter put it, "Our Western model of conventional economics assumes that every man maximizes his opportunities for higher income. But in backward societies it is not clear whether men seek a customary or an optimum standard of living. Less abstractly, if an Indian villager can grow on the same acreage twice as much wheat with the new varieties, will he work only half as long?" [4] In many ways the problems of improving UDC agriculture are closely related to those of "development" in general. The economy of the country must be generating the necessary capital and its educational system the required technicians. Otherwise these things must be supplied, at least in part, from outside. For the time being, there seems to be little alternative but for ODCs to lend massive assistance to UDCs in these areas, while simultaneously making an effort to help UDCs become capable of doing it themselves.

The United Nations has stated that all the UDCs together could not usefully absorb more than $20 billion in foreign aid each year. We cannot believe that these countries would be unable to use more than about $10 per capita in aid. Clearly much more could be spent constructively.

India, for example, could probably use ten million tons of fertilizers annually, which alone might cost $2–3 billion, or about 50 per cent of the maximum absorbable by that country under the U.N. estimate. And that figure does not include the cost of equipment for transporting or spreading the fertilizer. India also needs more extensive irrigation systems, better farm roads and, perhaps more importantly, better storage facilities. In 1968 the Indian Food and Agriculture Ministry estimated that almost 10 per cent of India's grain production was eaten by rats. Others think that the actual figure was 12 per cent. We would not be surprised if total wastage between harvest and table was normally 30 per cent or more.

[4] Nossiter, *Soft State*, p. 15.

Food losses between harvest and table are enormous in all UDCs. In two Philippine provinces in 1952–54, rats consumed 90 per cent of the sugar cane. Since 1960, the value of the annual toll of crops taken by birds in Africa has exceeded $7 million.

Aid to UDCs in constructing pest-proof food storage facilities would be one of the most intelligent possible forms of assistance that the ODCs could provide. Not only would it produce a substantial increase in the amount of food available for human consumption, but it would also cause a minimum of ecological problems. Tight facilities can be fumigated with short-lived pesticides which would not escape into ecosystems.

It seems certain that aid providing fertilizers, approved insecticides and herbicides, soil conditioners, storage facilities, farm-to-market roads and highways, trucks, tractors, combines, plows, hoes, rakes, wells, reservoirs, canals, pumps, pipes and other direct needs of UDC agriculture could utilize more than the UN figure of $10 per capita. If provision for the necessary research and development and trained agricultural extension workers are added in, the costs go up still further. This estimate does not even include other areas of economic aid, which UDCs will continue to need.

A great many research stations, patterned on the very successful International Rice Research Institute (IRRI) in the Philippines and the International Maize and Wheat Improvement Center (CIMMYT) in Mexico, must be established throughout the UDCs. Since most of these nations are in the tropics which are extremely diverse biologically with virtually every area posing unique agricultural problems, such research should be carried on locally as much as possible.

The provision of personnel for these stations and of agricultural technicians in general will require a massive effort. More people in both UDCs and ODCs will have to be persuaded or enticed into training for jobs as agronomists, agricultural technicians, and agricultural extension service personnel in UDCs. Skilled people from the ODCs will be needed to teach in agricultural training centers to be established in UDCs, and students from the UDCs must be brought to agricultural colleges in the United States or other ODCs for advanced training. This latter program will require both strengthening of agricultural schools and broadening their competence to develop and teach ecologically sound techniques of tropical agriculture. In addition, a strict policy must be adopted requiring the return of UDC trainees from ODCs to their native countries after completion of their education. Otherwise, "brain drain" problems will tend to undermine the programs.[5]

One advantage in selling such a full-scale agricultural aid program to the governments and citizens of ODCs is that a great deal of the money would be spent within them, expanding education facilities, producing fertilizers, manufacturing farm machinery, irrigation pumps, trucks and other equipment. But, as we have seen, aid in the agricultural sector alone will not suffice. UDC development in a more general sense is essential if the necessary demand for food is to be generated and if stable, reasonably self-sufficient economies are to evolve. Reform in the international trade situation would help a great deal toward this goal, as would massive population control efforts. But in most countries ways must also be found to upgrade non-agricultural segments of the economy in coordination with appropriate tariff changes to make foreign markets more attractive.

Planning for economic improvement often will deal with the unique problems of a given nation or area.

---

[5] The UDC-ODC brain drain does not result simply from Third World students lusting after the new life. Many of them return to their homelands and become frustrated in their attempts to apply newly acquired Western skills in a traditional society. When they find they cannot work effectively, they become discouraged and leave.

But some general principles must be widely recognized. Improving the life of the farmer or villager is a *sine qua non* of solving problems of urbanization. For as long as the lot of those living on the land is an unhappy one, the lure of the city will continue to draw unskilled people into urban slums. Ecological and resource considerations suggest a concentration of development programs in industries where the substitution of machine power for human labor is minimized. This does not necessarily mean the establishment of cottage industries. China's attempt at backyard steel mills, surely the most massive attempt ever made along these lines, was a dismal failure. Even on a more reasonable scale the failure rate of home handicraft industry schemes tends to be high. The Paddocks[6] pass on the report of a CARE official who supplied sewing machines and instruction in dressmaking to a southeast Asian village. Most of the women, once they had become seamstresses, left with their families for the city where they could make a better living!

It would seem more practical to establish such industries in centralized facilities where quality control can be maintained, tools shared, and goods marketed en masse. Clothing, simple farm implements (which presumably will be the main implements of labor-intensive farming), furniture and many other items would lend themselves to this type of operation. So would the assembly of bicycles, scooters, refrigerators and other devices from parts which could be imported.

Of course, an ideal export item for many UDCs would be fine hand-crafted goods or works of art—items whose creation involves massive amounts of skilled labor. Some Eskimo groups, especially those living in Ungava, have made a considerable success at marketing art work, especially soapstone carvings. These works, derived from their traditional art, have not only helped them to avoid the economic disaster which the white man has brought

---

[6] William and Paul Paddock, *Hungry Nations* (Boston: Little, Brown & Co., 1964), p. 123.

upon their fellows, but have helped them to keep alive their culture while enriching ours.

That is a limited success story, but perhaps there is some reason to hope that many people in ODCs, in an era of mass-produced junk, could learn to appreciate and take pride in owning the fine arts of other cultures. But, of course, just as every workman is not a Renoir, so every Eskimo is not a talented sculptor. Artistic talent is limited in all cultures, and opening of mass markets for high quality Eskimo seal skin stencils, aboriginal bark paintings, Bombara antelope masks, Latin American and Indian hand-dyed fabrics, and hand-loomed rugs from Kashmir and the Middle East would be just one small step in solving the general problem.

It could, however, be an important step, because it might also carry over to the rejuvenation of artisans in the ODCs. American hand-blown glass might have a huge resurgence (consider the interest already developed in old bottles, which belatedly have been recognized as often being things of beauty or of cultural-historical interest). We might also develop a preference for fine handmade furniture—an interest which clearly is latent, considering the thriving antique market. One wonders if the Japanese, now suffocating in filthy, overcrowded cities, might not wish they had concentrated on persuading everyone in the world to buy a netsuke instead of a transistor radio. *Netsuke,* the often intricately carved toggles used to secure items to the Japanese man's robe, could be useful items for almost everyone. One brand new netsuke, a carving of a group of turtles, recently sold in San Francisco for $2200, a price no one seems to have charged yet for a transistor portable!

Silly? Perhaps, but the basic idea is sound. People everywhere must abandon the pervasive idea that the components of a quality life are big, mass-produced, or packaged in plastic. The potential is there in the level of appreciation of fine art, books, jewelry, watches, cameras, wine and so forth that already exists among people. If we can increase that appreciation and lower the importance of new automobiles, and a constant turn-over of major appliances and heavy equipment in general, we will be accomplishing two things. We will be saving our life-support systems and improving the competitive positions of the UDCs, and thus improving the economic position of the UDCs as well.

In addition to economic problems, there are grave socio-political barriers in the path of the Green Revolution. Two of them, the prevalence of graft and the lack of progress toward land reform are problems whose solution must be generated by the citizens of the UDCs themselves.

Myrdal feels that the problem of the "soft state" is at least in part an unfortunate legacy of anarchic attitudes developed during colonial times which the new indigenous governments now find turned against themselves.[7] The habits of civil disobedience, non-cooperation and outright rebellion adopted during the struggles for independence still persist. These habits flourish along with the corruption that historically characterized many UDC governments and which is almost invariably a corollary of an illiterate, ill-informed, or deluded populace. Graft as a way of life is a very old story. This corruption is familiar to all UDC citizens, any observant traveler, and, indeed, any American who has read newspaper accounts of the politicians the U.S.A. supports in Saigon.

In 1968 S. Rajaratnoam, Indian Minister for Foreign Affairs and Labor, described the form of government as "kleptocracy" and said:

"It is amazing how otherwise excellent studies on development problems in Asia and Africa avoid any serious reference to the fact of corruption. It is not that the writers do not know of its existence but its relevance to the question of political stability and rapid economic development appears not to have been fully appreciated. It may also be that a serious probing of the subject

---

[7] Gunnar Myrdal, *The Challenge of World Poverty* (New York: Pantheon Books, 1970), p. 213.

has been avoided lest it should offend the sensibilities of Asians." [8]

In the UDCs with their traditional societies and a traditional system featuring "connections," large-scale graft and petty bribery with little loyalty to community or nation has thrived as an acceptable form in both business and government. Such a traditional system can only be honestly described as corrupt or irrational in a context of Western values even though the ODCs can hardly claim to be free of graft. The fact is, most ODCs recognize graft as an evil and such a Western context must be used. Western medicine and public health procedures have helped to create extreme overpopulation. Western economic goals are accepted by UDC governments and educational systems. Perhaps most important, Western-style organizational solutions are, at this time, the only kind known to mankind which offer any hope of ameliorating the coming crisis. Therefore, our discussion of this subject must be culture-bound.

Whatever its origins, kleptocracy was undoubtedly given a boost by the withdrawal of the colonialist's administrative power when independence was achieved. And corruption has tended to increase since independence. Ensuring that foreign aid reaches its intended recipients is made more difficult by corruption, which greatly weakens local respect for government and planning. It thus helps prevent the kind of coordinated intra- and international action so necessary to improving the general lot of people in the UDCs, which in turn is so necessary to the success of the Green Revolution and the survival of all of us.

Corruption and general governmental failure have also had the effect that little meaningful land reform has occurred in the UDCs. A farmer can hardly be expected to put out a maximum effort on land that he is share-cropping for an absentee landlord, unless he is at least permitted a substantial piece of the action. Lack

[8] Myrdal, *The Challenge of World Poverty*, p. 229.

of land reform[9] has already hurt the Green Revolution in India. The progressive farmers with large holdings have been in the best position to benefit from use of the new seeds; they had access to expertise and the capital for necessary inputs. The economic position of these progressives has improved relative to less fortunate farmers, and hard feelings have resulted. Moreover, some absentee landlords, lured by potential profits through high yields, have returned to the land, displacing their tenants and causing further trouble.

Out of 131 million agricultural workers in India, fully 30 million are landless. In addition, some 20 million of India's 49 million farms have less than 2.5 acres each and are considered too small for a successful farming operation. As a result, and in view of the failure of the government to institute badly needed reforms, rural unrest is increasing. Landless peasants have started a revolt, marauding, killing landlords, and forcibly occupying land.

In the first nine months of 1969 more than 300 parcels of land, amounting to a total of 100,000–300,000 acres, were seized. In one week in August 1970, *Time* Magazine[10] reported that some 32,000 acres in 10 of India's states were occupied by squatters; when they were removed, four people were killed and nine thousand arrested. A new splinter sect of the Indian communist party, the Naxalites (taking the name from a region in the Himalayas, Naxalbari) has been especially active in fomenting peasant rebellion, and has begun to execute landlords and other "class enemies." There has been a strong police reaction to the Naxalites, but

[9] Land reform may mean breaking up large estates (latifundia) and parceling out the land among the people working it. It may also mean the consolidation of small holdings into more efficient units. Both reforms are needed in many UDCs, as is tenancy reform—revision of the relationship between sharecroppers and landowners. Thus land reform is a whole complex of desirable changes in the relationships between the land and those who work and/or own it.

[10] *Time*, August 24, 1970.

the movement seems to be spreading and probably cannot be stopped by counter-violence. One suspects that only social justice in the shape of land reform will do the job. But such reforms will not be easy in a country with so many landless relative to the amount of land available, especially in view of the inability of the cities to satisfactorily absorb more people from rural areas.

It is not clear how much the ODCs can do to help UDCs rid themselves of corruption and institute land reform. Obviously the United States should stop supporting governments such as that of South Vietnam, where corruption goes far beyond traditional UDC standards simply because they are anti-communist. It has also been suggested that Western governments should strive to prevent their nationals from participating in the graft system of UDCs (greasing official palms with silver in those countries is now a way of life for European and American corporations). Such a move, however, seems exceedingly unlikely. If successful, the companies would quite likely cease to function ("When in Rome . . ."). Fundamentally, reforms must come from within. Perhaps the major contribution that could be made by the ODCs is to be open and frank about the need for such reforms, and to apply a maximum of moral pressure toward accomplishing them.

There is much more that ODCs can do in the area of education. Aside from agriculture-related education, there is a crying need for more elementary education (including adult education) and, in particular, for higher levels of literacy. Successful development will require understanding and coordinated efforts by the masses of people. It will also, hopefully, be accompanied by some form of political democracy. High levels of literacy are a prerequisite for both. The kinds of programs mentioned under education for population control can be used for attacking these more general goals and could absorb considerable aid from the ODCs.

Finally, under socio-political problems connected

with the Green Revolution, we must reiterate the need for assistance in raising standards of public health, including food aid to raise nutritional levels. Protein-starved and undernourished people do not make bright, active, productive farmers. Much of the presumed "laziness" of people in UDCs is due to disease and diet. Massive aid can be given by ODCs in these areas, but care must be taken. Improved public health means lower death rates (especially lowered child mortality) and thus more rapid population growth. Public health teams must operate to lower death *and birth* rates simultaneously. Secondly, any direct food aid must be given in ways which do not make people dependent on imported food (thus discouraging local agriculture). World supplies of surplus food, particularly high quality protein foods, are low in relation to need and will become even less adequate, so that assistance will be temporary at best.

Possibly the most serious problems facing the Green Revolution are not economic or socio-political, but biological. Huge monocultures of crops are being created and they are inherently unstable. Reserves of genetic variability in crops are being lost, and they are irreplaceable. Genetic variability is vital if crops are to be improved to provide resistance to ever-evolving pests. As now run, the Green Revolution requires agricultural inputs of pesticides and fertilizers which have serious ecological effects both inside and outside the agricultural ecosystems.

A point very often ignored is that the climate and soil conditions of the tropics usually produce conditions less congenial to agriculture than those of the temperate zones. Consequently, the environments of most UDCs doubtless will not prove as receptive to the techniques used in ODCs as did ODC environments. Farming in the tropics is a much tougher proposition than farming in the temperate zones. Soil is usually poorer, and competition from pests generally is both more intense and more difficult to combat.[11] Considering the reluctance of ODC agriculturalists to change their behavior in the face of gross ecological threats, it is perhaps presumptuous to suggest that ODCs could help UDCs with their agricultural problems! Clearly, the time has come for biologists in many subdisciplines to turn their attention to the general problems of ecologically sound agriculture producing the highest possible yields, paying special attention to yields of high quality protein and to the special problems of tropical agriculture.

We are already in a position to supply certain badly-needed forms of aid. For instance, more strain "banks" could be established in various parts of the world to assure the maintenance of adequate genetic variability in our crop plants. Such banks are already in operation in the United States, Soviet Union, and elsewhere, but they are inadequate. Banks could be set up along with UDC agricultural experiment stations.

The ODCs could also quickly train large numbers of people in the techniques of integrated pest control and send them as advisors to UDCs. Integrated control does not attempt the hopeless task of pest eradication through use of pesticides in massive spray programs. Instead, it relies on careful evaluation of the situation, including establishment of a level of pest abundance that does not cause unacceptable damage to crops. Then one or more of a variety of control measures may be used: cultural, biological, or chemical. An example of cultural control would be to destroy plants near fields which harbor a pest when it is not attacking the crops. Biological controls usually involve the use of predators or disease organisms to attack a pest, but techniques such as releasing sterilized male pests to mate with

---

[11] An excellent summary of the difficulties of farming the tropics is given by Dr. Daniel Janzen, the foremost tropical ecologist, in *Bulletin, Ecological Society America*, vol. 51, no. 3, pp. 4-7. The same problems, seen through the eyes of a farmer, are summarized by Darry G. Cole in the April 22 issue of the *National Observer* (quoted in Ehrlich and Ehrlich, *Population, Resources, Environment*, pp. 92-93).

female pests are also biological controls. And, of course, chemical controls do not necessarily mean broadcast use of long-lasting poisons. Pesticides that break down quickly and do not accumulate in ecological systems may be employed locally when other methods fail.

The need for trained technicians is more acute if ecologically sensible control methods are used than if sprays are used by the calendar, as is now so often the practice in ODC agriculture. Under the calendar-spray system the farmer simply applies a given quantity of poison per acre on specified dates, regardless of whether pests are present or not. This method wastes pesticide, increases the likelihood that the pest will become resistant, and exterminates the pest's natural enemies. Therefore, the farmer becomes more and more dependent on increasingly potent pesticides to control them. Needless to say, the sequence means immense profits for the petrochemical industry, which vigorously promotes it. Everyone else loses. The farmer pays much more to control pests, often with poor results. The housewife pays more for her produce and often gets low-level pesticide poisoning in the bargain. And we all lose as the life-support systems of the planet deteriorate.

Using integrated control in either ODCs or UDCs, on the other hand, would involve some very high initial costs. Technicians must be trained to evaluate pest populations and to design control methods, and these technicians would have to pass on their knowledge to the farmers. In addition, the present dependence on pesticides has damaged or destroyed many natural controls over pests. It has created an unstable situation which will require both great care and considerable expense during the transition to intelligent control methods in order to avert further damage to ecological systems. High yield agriculture is now "hooked" on pesticides as an addict is hooked on heroin. Withdrawal must be carefully handled and will have a high cost, but withdrawal is necessary for survival. Lester Brown, one of the prime movers of the Green Revolution, summarized the central problem of producing more food very well.[12]

"Whatever measures are taken there is growing doubt that the agricultural ecosystem will be able to accommodate both the anticipated increase of the human population to seven billion by the end of the century and the universal desire of the world's hungry for a better diet. The central question is no longer 'Can we produce enough food?' but 'What are the environmental consequences of attempting to do so?'"

In conclusion, the ODCs can make enormous contributions to the improvement of UDC agriculture, but it will require both a will to help and a willingness to recognize and rectify the errors now being made in ODC agriculture. Time is short, and every day wasted dooms more people to death by starvation.

---

[12] *Scientific American,* September, 1970, p. 170.

VI

Control Systems

As the population grows ever larger and our spaceship is ever more threatened, it becomes increasingly obvious that governments have lost control of events. Where at one time kings, presidents, legislators, emperors, mayors and other officials seemed able to make decisions aimed at avoiding disaster, this often is no longer the case. The President of the United States is helpless, or unwilling, in the face of a war economy (and the power of those sustained by it) to terminate a ghastly, useless, and immoral war. The leaders of the Soviet Union risk the end of civilization to press Russia's parochial interests in the Middle East. Japan's prime minister calls for a higher birthrate for his nation, a nation already undergoing a catastrophic deterioration of its environment, in part because of overpopulation. India and Pakistan, both facing massive famine and disease and each with per capita gross national products of under $100, use their limited energy and resources to make war.

The evidence of governmental failure is everywhere. At a time when we should be cutting back the contribution of manufacturing to the Gross National Product and expanding services, Governor Reagan of California launches an all-out war on some of the state's services; the system of higher education and the mental health apparatus. At a time when most people are looking to science to prolong their lives, provide solutions to pollution problems and find new ways to raise food production, President Nixon permits precipitous withdrawal of federal support for science (when what was needed was leadership toward a vast reordering of scientific priorities). And, while legislators, often in the pay of polluters, scramble to give speeches in defense of the environment, a joint House-Senate committee lops $500,000 off the pitiful $1,500,000 budget of the President's captive Council on Environmental Quality. They did not cut the budget because they recognized that the role and personnel of the Council were arranged so as to guarantee it would be a toothless pussycat rather than a tiger. *That* might have been a hopeful sign. Instead, they did it in the name of economy—during a session when many billions had been appropriated for useless or dangerous toys for the military and the airline industry. Local governments, too, seem incapable of orienting to reality. Under pressure from real estate developers and other irresponsible groups they often try to encourage population growth and industrialization "in order to broaden the tax base and lower taxes." They either do not know or do not care that population growth and industrialization tend to generate *higher* individual tax loads, not lower.

It seems that at every level, governments cannot provide what governments must provide: rational collective action to achieve beneficial results unattainable by individual action. City government cannot provide a citizen safe passage down city streets after dark. State government cannot prevent air pollution or provide adequate care for ill, indigent or antisocial citizens. Federal government cannot control the military, change Alice-in-Wonderland foreign policies or guarantee the rights of blacks, Chicanos, American Indians or women. The United Nations cannot even keep Israelis and Arabs from killing each other, let alone provide any kind of leadership towards a healthy, peaceful globe.

Is there any way in which the situation might be changed? Can mankind somehow change it attitudes enough to reorganize itself so that governments begin again to move toward the ideals which, alas, they have all-too-rarely approached in the past? The answer is that we must because we have no choice. The world is too crowded and too complex for anarchy, and too diverse for a worldwide dictatorship. We would not presume in this chapter to offer solutions which have eluded Homo sapiens for many thousands of years. We cannot conjure up some kind of ideal design for world governance. But we can point out the way in which some of the structural problems of government might be solved —ways in which a new breed of men might attempt to control their affairs for the common good. But we would be among the first to proclaim that without the new men no structural change will function. The possible emergence of new men will be discussed in the next chapter.

Governmental Reforms in the United States

As Americans, it behooves us first to examine needed changes in our own government. We know more about it, and we can personally *do* more about it. We are, furthermore, fortunate in that the U.S.A. is closely observed by the other nations of the Earth. Therefore, reforms instituted here will have effects far beyond our borders.

Consider some of the major structural faults in the U.S. Federal Government. First of all, the legislature, especially the House of Representatives, is designed to represent parochial rather than national interests. This situation may have been suitable for an eighteenth century confederation, but is hardly suitable for a modern nation. In addition, the legislature in large part has come to represent not the people as a whole, but special interests able to spend large amounts of money to inform, persuade or buy outright congressmen and senators. Within the legislature, a system of seniority has concentrated power in the hands of elderly committee chairmen, men who, even when they are honest, tend to be out of touch with the realities of a rapidly changing world.

All is not well in the Executive Branch, either. As the responsibilities of the President have increased, the power to act constructively has diminished. Modern communications have placed many decisions that used to be made by ambassadors, generals or admirals in the field in the hands of the President. President Johnson, for instance, is reported to have decided personally how many sorties against North Vietnam would be flown by U.S. aircraft on a day-to-day basis. President Kennedy followed the Cuban missile crisis on a minute-to-minute basis, ready at any time to make a decision which could have meant the end of civilization.

On the domestic front the Twenty-second Amendment to the Constitution has weakened the power of the President to get badly needed legislation through the Congress. This amendment, preventing a President from serving more than two terms greatly reduces his political clout during the second term (but also removes some of the political pressure on him, which could permit more courageous leadership). Furthermore, much of the business of the Executive Branch is carried out in a vast bureaucracy of departments and agencies. Neither the President nor any other responsible official has any real control over this bureaucracy.

The organizations of the Executive Branch mostly function as independent empires, often at cross purposes with one another and always under the strong influence or outright control of the interests they purport to regulate. The Department of Agriculture (or, as it should more accurately be named, the Department of Agribusiness) has long played footsie with the petrochemical industry, promoting exceedingly dangerous and guaranteed-to-fail pest control procedures in order to maintain the profits of the industry—to the detriment of all Americans, particularly farmers. While the Department of Health, Education and Welfare attempts unsuccessfully to keep Americans healthy, the Department of Agriculture promotes the use of dangerous agricultural chemicals and feeds fat and starch to the poor who are protein-starved.

Perhaps the most dangerous single agency outside of the Department of Defense (DOD) is the Atomic Energy Commission (AEC) which has, among other duties, the impossible task of both promoting and regulating the peaceful uses of atomic energy. Under pressure from the power industry and at the urging of a group of guilt-laden physicists, the AEC emphasizes promotion, and has a dismal record at regulation. The physicists, horrified at the first uses to which men put nuclear power, have zealously tried to show that the same power could be a vast benefit to mankind. The result has been the AEC's promotion of a long series of schemes, virtually all premature or completely unworkable, which would lead to irreversible radioactive poisoning of our planet.

The collusion between the Department of Defense (DOD) and the industrialists who supply arms is so blatant and well-known so as to require no further comment here. The Ralph Nader Study Group Report by Robert Fellmeth on the Interstate Commerce Commission was entitled *The Interstate Commerce Omission*. It documented in great detail the stupidity and total lack of concern for the public interest of this agency, which is owned lock, stock and barrel by the railroad, trucking, shipping and pipeline industries. Similar stories could be told about most units of the executive bureaucracy.

We are a long way from establishing anything remotely resembling a Department of Population and Environment such as was discussed earlier. The need for unified, public-interest-oriented planning and regulation is obvious. A DPE should include the functions of all of these organizations: Bureau of the Census, Department of the Interior, Federal Air Pollution Control Administration, National Oceanic and Atmospheric Administration, and the Council on Environmental Quality. It should, of course, have more power over the private sector and state and local governments than all of these combined. Furthermore, it should have absolute veto power over many of the activities of the Department of Defense (especially the Army Corps of Engineers), Atomic Energy Commission, Department of Agriculture, Federal Power Commission, Interstate Commerce Commission, Federal Aviation Administration, Federal Trade Commission, Federal Communications Commission, and Federal Highway Commission.

The Judicial Branch has its problems, too. The Supreme Court now substitutes its opinions for an out-of-date Constitution. Many of the structural problems mentioned in connection with the legislative and executive branches can be traced to the inadequacies of a document written in 1787 (for a loose confederation of agrarian states with a total of less than four million people) and still being used as the fundamental law of a late-twentieth century industrial state with a population of more than 200 million. The Constitution was written for a people living on the edge of an "empty" continent, a continent now filled. It was also written to protect people from government, and says almost nothing about the obligations people have to the government, obligations which become more and more important as society grows more crowded and complex.

The campaigning process as it now functions gives enormous advantages to wealthy candidates or those willing to sell out for financial support, but there is no constitutional control over this process. In the 1968 election, Richard Nixon was elected because he had the financial backing and patience to be merchandized on television like a deodorant.[1] In the 1970 New York

---

[1] The details can be obtained from Joe McGinniss' fascinating book, *The Selling of the President 1968* (New York: Trident Press, 1968). One of the few encouraging aspects of the 1970 election was the relative lack of success of TV promotion of candidates. Perhaps Americans are learning that TV ads about candidates are no more reliable than ads for products.

gubernatorial race, super-rich Governor Rockefeller was able to hire over 350 full-time campaign personnel. His unsuccessful challenger, Arthur Goldberg, could hire only about 30.

Finally, but not exhaustively, there is no agency in our government charged with long-range planning for the entire nation.

One route to the structural changes required in our government could be through reform or replacement of the 1787 Constitution. Unfortunately this presents us with another structural problem. The amendment procedure for the Constitution rests in the hands of the most retrograde of our governmental bodies, the United States Congress and the legislatures of the 50 states. Amendments have been few and far between, 15 in some 180 years since the first ten (the Bill of Rights) were passed in the year the Constitution went into effect. The procedure is much too cumbersome, and it seems unlikely that the legislatures will voluntarily give up their power and make it less so.

There was, of course, no provision put in the 1787 Constitution for its replacement when changed circumstances made such replacement prudent. If there is any power to replace the Constitution, it clearly rests with the people, who are the ultimate source of all power to govern.

If a way could be found to replace the old Constitution, what form might a new Constitution take? One of the major projects of the Center for the Study of Democratic Institutions has been the drafting of a model for a new American Constitution. The prime mover of the project has been Rexford G. Tugwell, formerly a professor of economics at Columbia, a member of Franklin Delano Roosevelt's famous "brain trust," Roosevelt's Under-Secretary of Agriculture, head of the planning department of the New York City Planning Commission, and Governor of Puerto Rico. The 37th draft version of Tugwell's "Constitution for a United

Republic of America" is printed as Appendix III to this book. (See page 166.)

The Tugwell Constitution is intended only to serve as a model for discussion—a role for which it is eminently suited. There is in the draft an attempt to deal with the various structural problems mentioned above, and more. For instance, there is a Planning Branch of the government (Article III), which would do comprehensive long-term planning for the government. Instead of today's chaotic and extra-constitutional regulatory agencies there would be a Regulatory Branch of Government. The President would be relieved of the impossible duties of running a huge Executive Branch, and regulatory power would be centralized with appropriate safeguards to prevent the "capture" of regulatory bodies by those they are supposed to regulate.

As a further safeguard against corruption in the Regulatory Branch or elsewhere in the government, a nationally (rather than parochially) based senate would elect a "Watchkeeper." The Watchkeeper is charged with gathering and organizing information "concerning the adequacy, competence, and integrity of governmental agencies and their personnel, as well as their continued usefulness; he shall also suggest the need for new or expanded services; and he shall also report concerning any agency, the deleterious effect of its activities on citizens or on the environment."

The section on the House of Representatives (Article V B) deserves careful study. Note, for example, the provision for selection of committee chairmen from at-large members, and the limit of six years put on the tenure of such chairmen.

Many, if not most, people will disagree with parts of the model Constitution. Some will prefer a more profound change—say, to a parliamentary system. Some will not like the elitist Senate. Civil libertarians may be worried that a "Bill of Rights" is not present under that rubric, or that the Electoral Branch will not be able adequately to prevent unscrupulous manipulating of elections. Conservatives may oppose it on principle. We disagree with many of its features, major and minor. For example, we would like to see Article V B section 9 (A) changed to provide that the House shall have the duty "to enact such measures as will assure that the population of the United Republic remain at an optimum level, using estimates made by the Planning Board concerning resources and the general well-being of all peoples."

We reiterate, however, that the Tugwell Constitution is designed as a model for discussion—not as a replacement for the 1787 Constitution. This leads us to the question of the value of such a model. For one thing, discussion of it could lead large numbers of Americans to a realization of the shortcomings of our Constitution and the resultant inadequacies of our government. This might provide a climate of opinion in which a new Constitutional Convention might be possible. Tugwell (CM III, 5, p. 24) himself suggests that a strong President, near the end of his term "provoked by his inability to move the Congress, determined to check the government's hardening into bureaucratic stolidity, fearful of the accumulating consequences of obsolescence, and conscious of his inability to carry all his responsibilities, concludes that he must appeal for consent to a new constitution." It is conceivable that in the crisis years ahead we will get such an extraordinary President, although the prospects in 1970, as this is written, seem dim indeed. It is even possible that the American people would accede to his request and that a modern, workable Constitution which thoroughly protected our civil liberties would result.

We contend, however, that no such result is likely in the current atmosphere of repression, distrust and hatred. Minority groups, for instance, would distrust the motives of the majority in acquiescing to a Constitutional Convention—and with good reason. Indeed a Constitutional Convention could prove to be extremely divisive and could undermine what little credibility and legitimacy the present governmental authority retains. To identify the diverse interests of over 205 million people and mold them into a coherent document would require a climate of unity and compromise under *any* circumstances. Our country is at present moving away from such a climate, so it seems doubtful if the population-environment movement would be well advised to dissipate its energy working for a Constitutional Convention. The achievement of a state where constitutional reform is feasible will probably mean that the battle for survival has been already won on other fronts.

At the moment, then, a move toward a new Constitution is unlikely, to say the least. This is probably just as well, considering the tenor of the country. But a thorough airing of the faults of the old Constitution now should be beneficial anyway. At least it might lead to a situation where legislatures will be forced to pass some badly needed amendments, or, at the very least, it might make resistance lighter if the day ever comes when new men call for a new Constitution.

International Controls

Bad as things are with respect to the internal affairs of the United States, they seem a miracle of perfection in contrast to our international dealings and the activities of other nations of Spaceship Earth. True, at home we let the poor starve, force our non-white citizens to live degraded lives, concentrate our medical care on the affluent, teach our children that sexual enjoyment is bad and that killing is permissible, and poison our bodies, minds and environment.

But since the Second World War the United States has, along with the Soviet Union, England, France and China, played nuclear dice with the very survival of humanity, while establishing a "rich man's club" which has proceeded to exploit the poor two-thirds of the world. The war in Vietnam is simply the latest and grossest example of such exploitation.

While the control systems of the United States and other ODCs are inadequate to the needs of the late 20th century, an international control system is in any real sense nonexistent. No international control was applied to prevent the Soviet Union from crushing Czechoslovakia. The world community was helpless to prevent the United Arab Republic and its allies from threatening Israel with genocide, and it was equally unable to protect the Arab nations from the Israeli response. No police agency could be called to save the children of Biafra or to end the conflict between India and Pakistan. Tibet was conquered by the People's Republic of China, and nothing could be done. And, of course, the United States has treated the world to the drawn-out spectacle of the world's mightiest nation systematically murdering the people of Indochina and destroying the environmental fabric of the area in order to save the faces of incompetent militarists and politicians and to keep American fingers in the rich resource pie of Southeast Asia.[2] There is no international government that will keep American boys from being sent to far corners of the world to die protecting the interests of such large corporations as Ling-Temco-Vought, Chase Manhattan Bank or Standard Oil, to mention

[2] As Senator Dale McGee said, "Southeast Asia is the last major resource area outside the control of any one of the major powers of the globe." The theme of "making the world safe for American investment" is recurrent in big business. The Economic Research Division of the Chase Manhattan Bank stated, "Thailand promises to be an excellent investment and sales area for Americans if rebel insurgency can be contained." With five billion dollars to be spent on oil exploration in Southeast Asia in the next dozen years (*Time*, April 12, 1970) it seems inevitable that an American "presence" in that area will be "required" into the indefinite future. For further information on the role of resources in our Indochina war, see Gabriel Kolko's *The Roots of American Foreign Policy* (Boston: Beacon Press, 1969), particularly Chapter 4.

only a few. No sanctions are applied to those directly or indirectly responsible for the death in battle of young men from Hanoi, Lagos, Taipei, Sydney, Cairo, Amman, Srinigar, Seoul, Karachi or Los Angeles. Moreover, the people of the world do not determine democratically how their precious stores of petroleum, copper, uranium and other nonrenewable resources are to be utilized. There is no regulatory agency to keep nations from decimating oceanic fisheries, to prevent one nation from causing deleterious changes in the weather of another, or to prevent one or more nations from irreversibly poisoning the ecological systems upon which all human life depends.

Clearly if civilization is to persist, this chaotic international situation cannot be permitted to continue. Spaceship Earth must function as a single entity; international controls must exist in several areas. It is simple to outline what is necessary: control of production and sales of arms, followed by control of international conflict; regulation of trade, resource utilization and environmental impact; and control of population. Needless to say, the institution of these controls will not be simple; it represents the most elusive of goals.

Attempts at simply establishing world government have failed. The League of Nations and later the United Nations have both been unable to accomplish even their most elementary aims, the ending of war. The reasons for their failure are complex, but we can boil them down to one central cause: the failure of most people and nations to recognize the nature of the planetary commons. Garrett Hardin, in his already classic paper, "The Tragedy of the Commons,"[8] carefully analyzes the results of joint utilization of a commons. He points out that if a group of herdsmen use a common pasture, the optimum strategy for each seems to be to increase his herd as rapidly as possible. And that *is* his best strategy for the short term. But in the long run growth of the herds

---

[8] Garrett Hardin, "The Tragedy of the Commons," *Science* 162 (1968): 1243-1248.

leads to over-grazing which destroys the carrying capacity of the pasture. Then all the herdsmen are out of business.

The world ecosystem in aggregate should be thought of as a gigantic commons. Men draw on it for resources such as food, minerals and oxygen. They utilize the same commons as a dump for their wastes. Parts of the world ecosystem are under private or national control (and thus cannot legally be part of an international commons); the majority of the world commons consists of oceans and atmosphere which cannot be fenced off by individuals or nations. However, the international trade system (backed by ODC military and economic power) comes close to converting many of the resources that occur within national boundaries into part of the international commons. UDCs, with the "legal" right to withhold resources from a functional common pool, may find it impossible to do so in practice.

The profligate looting of the oceans of their protein, and the uncaring use of them as the ultimate planetary cesspool are classic examples of mistreatment of a commons. So is the accelerating destruction and dispersal of the Earth's nonrenewable resources. The inevitable end is eloquently stated by Hardin: "Ruin is the destination toward which all men rush, each pursuing his own best interest in a society that believes in the freedom of the commons. *Freedom in a commons brings ruin to all.*" That is precisely what will happen as men and nations race to extract a maximum of private and national benefits from the planetary commons.

Hardin argues persuasively that the only hope for dealing with the problem of the commons is "mutual coercion, mutually agreed upon." One should not be instantly repelled by the term coercion. Appeals for the voluntary exercise of restraint in relation to the commons have proven notoriously ineffective. We do not pay our taxes on the honor system, nor do we permit each person to harvest all the fish or game he desires, merely asking him to behave "responsibly" and not to take too many. We apply mutually agreed upon sanctions to those who evade taxes or take more than their limit of fishes. Hardin argues that an appeal to responsibility puts an individual in a hopeless double bind. On one hand, it produces fear of societal disapproval if he does not behave in the proper way towards the commons. On the other hand, it produces the fear that if he restrains himself others will take advantage and exploit the commons more.

Hardin extends his analysis to the area of population control, considering the carrying capacity of the Earth for human beings as a commons. Each person, when he or she has a child, uses up a bit of this commons. At present all informed people agree that the planet is overpopulated, and they know that runaway population growth must be halted if unprecedented disaster is to be avoided. As a result, pleas for responsible reproductive behavior are repeatedly voiced (we have voiced a few ourselves). In spite of this, there has been very little sign that people are restraining themselves reproductively for the public good. In fact the most commonly voiced fear is that other people (or other groups) will outreproduce those showing restraint.

How then might we develop the badly needed international controls—the mutual coercion mutually agreed upon—needed to protect the planetary commons and thus our very lives? We must put a maximum effort into achieving such controls in spite of the record of dismal failure in the past. If nothing else, the unprecedented and increasing seriousness of the current situation should continually convince more and more people of the need to bring an end to anarchy among nations. A first step, of course, is the creation of a climate of opinion within nations which favors some relinquishment of sovereignty of national governments. The citizens of the United States and Soviet Union must understand, among other things, that the effluent they pour into the oceans and the weapons systems they construct are the legitimate objects of control by supra-national government. The

Arab countries must come to realize that their oil reserves are a vital resource for all humanity, and that the use of those reserves is the proper subject of regulation. All nations must come to view nonrenewable resources as being held in trust for all mankind, present and future. And all mankind must have a say in their use.

It will indeed be a giant step to convince a substantial portion of humanity that the Earth is a commons and that exercising free access to the commons (either as individuals or nations) leads to disaster for all. But such an educational process is absolutely essential if men are to accept a truly functional international control system.

A good place to start that process in America would be in educating our citizens about the massive warfare state which we have created. A major responsibility for the nuclear arms race rests squarely on our doorstep. Those who do not accept this statement are referred to an impeccable source, Dr. Herbert York. Dr. York has been involved in the defense establishment since World War II. He served as Director of Defense Research and Engineering under Presidents Eisenhower and Kennedy, and was involved with most of the critical governmental committees working on defense problems in the late 1950's and early 1960's. In a superb book, *Race to Oblivion: A Participant's View of the Arms Race*, he tells a horrifying story of the honest mistakes, stupidity, venality, jingoism and bureaucratic bungling which have brought us (with a parallel contribution from the Soviet Union) ever closer to a thermonuclear Armageddon.

Although the details of the arms race are widely available, we know of no more compelling account than York's book. He summarizes the results of the race as twin ultimate absurdities.

"The first of these absurdities has been with us for some time, and has come to be widely recognized for what it is. It lies in the fact that ever since World War II the military power of the United States has been steadily increasing, while at the same time our national security has been rapidly and inexorably decreasing. The same thing is happening to the Soviet Union.

"The second of these absurdities is still in an early stage and, for reasons of secrecy, is not yet so widely recognized as the first. It lies in the fact that in the United States the power to decide whether or not the doomsday has arrived is in the process of passing from statesmen and politicians to lower-level officials and technicians and, eventually, to machines. Presumably, the same thing is happening in the Soviet Union.[4]

Well, there you have it. Ballistic missiles with MIRVs (multiple independently targeted re-entry vehicles) and the construction of anti-ballistic missile (ABM) systems are leading us to the point where military reactions will have to occur virtually instantly. Soon the power to decide whether civilization, perhaps humanity itself, will live or die will be vested in a computer. Keep in mind that computers are machines which, contrary to the advertising of computer manufacturers, are notorious for malfunctioning. But when they do work they operate so swiftly that they are difficult or impossible to countermand.

How are we to make the average American or Russian recognize the hideous trap into which he is being lured by ambitious military men and defense scientists, profit-motivated industrialists, confused politicians, and nervous party functionaries? Consider the attitudes of some average American citizens on the arms race and Vietnam, recently expressed on nationwide TV:[5]

"I have absolute faith in the Pentagon. I believe they are the only ones qualified to set their budget . . ." "We should drop the atom bomb . . ." "The guy who yells peace is the guy who always gets war . . ." "Seventy-

---

[4] Herbert York, *Race to Oblivion* (New York: Simon and Schuster, 1970), p. 228.

[5] Quoted from Harlan Ellison, *The Glass Teat* (New York: Ace Books, 1970), p. 250.

seven billion for armaments? I'm in favor of it . . ." "It's
the liberal Mafia that keeps this (Vietnam) war from
being won."

The touching faith of these "common men" in the
perspicacity and motivation of the military and their
buddies is a crushing indictment of our educational system. It is also a tribute to the propaganda of those who
wish to see the resources of our society wasted on
dangerous armaments. Contrast their faith in the militarists with this statement by an informed person, Dr.
York:[6] "The hard-sell technologists and their syco-
phants invented the term 'missile gap,' and they em-
bellished that simple phrase with ornate horror stories
about imminent threats to our very existence as a nation." As York points out, the military-industrial complex then invented extremely complex and expensive
cures for the missile gap and reviled anyone who sought
to interrupt the resultant flow of gold and power to them
as "unable to understand the situation, technically backward, and trying to put the budget ahead of survival."
The missile gap was of course purely imaginary, as have
been numerous other "threats" invented by these fan-
tasy-prone people.

The United States does not make its only contribution to the fight against peace in its role as a continual
escalator of the nuclear arms race. Since World War II
we have also become the major source of the conventional arms that have been used to fight more than 50
sizeable wars since 1945. Consider the words of George
Thayer, author of a detailed study of the international
trade in non-nuclear armaments.[7] Mr. Thayer, judging
from his use of slogans such as "the free world" and his
frequent condemnation of the arms deals of communist
countries, is no "communist dupe." Yet he writes:[8]

---

[6] York, Race to Oblivion, p. 11.

[7] George Thayer, The War Business (New York: Avon Books,
1969).

[8] Thayer, The War Business, p. 376.

"Still, today's arms trade is essentially an American problem. No nation talks more loudly about peace, yet no nation distributes as many weapons of war. No nation has spoken so passionately in favor of nuclear controls, yet no nation has been so silent of the subject of conventional arms controls. Nor has any nation been as vocal in its desire to eradicate hunger, poverty and disease, yet no nation has so obstructed the fight against these ills through its insistence that poor countries waste their money on expensive and useless arms."

If we are so far ahead of other nations in this area, it is not for their lack of trying to catch up. Perhaps the situation was best summarized by Joan Baez: "We are not the worst, we are only the biggest."

Warnings about the dangers of the arms race and the power of the military-industrial complex have been voiced repeatedly and loudly in the United States from a vast diversity of sources. President Eisenhower, in his farewell address, was the first and to date the only President to caution against the growing influence of the complex, warning that "public policy could itself become the captive of a scientific-technological elite." Presumably every literate American should be aware that now the military-industrial complex has become the most powerful force in our society and is using its influence to drive us down the road to thermonuclear war. And, as York so eloquently demonstrates, we are on the verge of turning public policy over not only to a scientific-technological elite, but to the computers (or pre-programed military men) produced by that elite.

Why has not the public, over the past decade, risen up and simply called the whole miserable shambles to a halt? One reason is that only a very small number of Americans are sufficiently well-informed to understand the situation in any depth. Another is that two successive Presidents, Johnson and Nixon, have suffered from an inordinate respect for the opinions of self-seeking generals, defense scientists, and industrialists. Neither has offered leadership in curbing the activities of the military-industrial complex or in informing the American people about the true nature of the threat facing our nation.[9] What is perhaps even sadder, most of the other "Presidential possibilities" now mentioned as probable opponents of Nixon in 1972 do not seem to have the qualities necessary to win, combined with a grasp of the central issues before us and a desire to take dramatic action to deal with them.

Nowhere more than in the area of political leadership is the need for new men more obvious. The next President of the United States had better be an extraordinary leader, for among his main tasks will be to rally the American people and break the power of the military-industrial complex.[10] He will have to guide a massive change in attitudes towards what constitutes national security. As the leader of the most powerful nation in the world, the new President must also play a prominent role in persuading other nations to pursue a course leading to effective international control of armaments.

If Americans can be brought to understand the significance of the warfare state and its counterpart in the Soviet Union, then they should be much more receptive to the necessity for some form of international government. They will realize that opting for ever more over-

[9] President Kennedy was certainly not blameless in this area, but his assassination came at a time when indications were that he was learning fast about the military. Whether he would have tried to limit the power of the complex is an open question. It would have been a monumental, perhaps impossible, task even for a man of his intelligence and popularity.

[10] We agree with the many authors who have claimed that the military-industrial complex (or military-industrial-government-university complex) is not a conscious conspiracy to destroy the United States and the world. Rather, it is an epiphenomenon of a grasping, alienated, dehumanized culture run by and for administrators and a small ruling class. We can expect the individuals concerned to be no more or less moral by the standards of our society than the average uninvolved citizen. What must be done is to rid ourselves of the old standards; "do unto others before they do unto you" is no longer an ethic for survival.

kill in a situation of international anarchy will lead inevitably to disaster. This should result in a groundswell of opinion favoring an end to that anarchy.

In our opinion, the course most likely to produce an effective global control system would be a stepwise acceptance of the realities of the world commons. For instance, a small start has already been made toward the establishment of an "Ocean Regime"—an institution charged with the development of a code of conduct for all nations, non-governmental entities, and individuals who utilize the sea. Under the auspices of the Center for the Study of Democratic Institutions, a meeting for control of the oceans was held at Malta in the summer of 1970. There was strong agreement at the conference that all the oceans must be placed under international control, and there was considerable discussion of how such controls might be set up. We hope that this first halting step will be followed quickly by further meetings; the United States could perform a great service to humanity by offering the United Nations a no-strings-attached grant to finance them.

As the decade of the 1970's proceeds, the need for international control of the oceans will become more and more apparent. Unless the world is extraordinarily fortunate, per capita (and perhaps absolute) fisheries catches will be decreasing dramatically, and conflict among fishing nations will be escalating in response. The most recent signs are ominous. In 1969 the world suffered its first absolute loss in fisheries yield since 1950. The loss was 1 per cent in the overdeveloped countries, 5 per cent in the underdeveloped. Since world population *grew* 2 per cent during the same period, the per capita loss was even larger. This loss was particularly serious in the light of the increased fishing effort that was made. If 1969 was the harbinger of a new trend, the end may be much closer than we suspected—and the approach of that end will focus attention on the tragedy of the ocean commons.

Furthermore, as access to land-based resources becomes more and more difficult, attempts to extract those of the continental shelf and the deep sea bed will greatly increase human activity in the seas, and along with it, the chances of conflict over use of the commons. One may also expect technology further to destabilize the nuclear arms race during the next decade, by solving the difficult technological problem of accurate long-range submarine detection.[11] The instability inherent in the MIRV-ABM developments will then be exacerbated with possibly catastrophic consequences. But at least when this event occurs, both the U.S.A. and Soviet Union will have much smaller vested interests in blocking effective international control of the ocean commons. Either through the United Nations or through some entirely new agency, regulation of human activities in the oceans might be imposed, complete with appropriate sanctions and an international navy for patrol and enforcement, thus providing alternative and productive uses for some of the ships and men of the world's navies. Other naval units, especially helicopter carriers, might be converted into floating aid stations for supplying food, health and contraceptive services, and technical expertise to the UDCs, as was foreshadowed in the aftermath of the 1970 Peruvian earthquake.

Bringing the oceans under international control would

---

[11] Up to now, the United States has maintained a fairly constant edge over the Soviet Union in the overall balance in strategic arms. Although the Intercontinental Ballistic Missile (ICBM) forces of both nations were roughly even at the end of the 1960's, the U.S. had over four times as many heavy bombers capable of striking the Soviet Union from American bases and had an even greater advantage in submarine-launched ballistic missiles (SLBMs)—656 for us to slightly over 100 for the U.S.S.R. Should the Soviets develop the capability of spotting the 40 or so submarines carrying our SLBMs, their problems in making a counter force strike against our nuclear weapons will be greatly reduced. They will by then have many or all of their ICBMs equipped with multiple independently-targeted reentry vehicles (MIRVs), making it possible for a single ICBM simultaneously to attack a series of targets with thermonuclear bombs. An expenditure of a relatively small portion of their ICBM force might completely remove our SLBM force.

be a giant step towards controlling the entire world commons. For instance, most oceanic pollution results from pollutants being washed from the continents or from pollutants settling from the atmosphere. Furthermore, interactions at the atmosphere-ocean interface are important determinants of weather. Control over human activities on continents and in the atmosphere is therefore critical to saving the oceans, and vice versa. Once the step of limiting freedom in the ocean commons is taken, similar steps for protecting other planetary commons could follow rapidly.

We feel, then, that if there is to be a real hope of instituting international government, the best chance lies in a stepwise extension of controls. We have already had some small steps towards control of outer space and the Antarctic. The big barrier will be governing the oceans. If we can accomplish that, the rest of the world may be brought under international control relatively easily.

VII

The Spacemen

WE MUST NOW examine the most difficult problem facing us as we try to save our endangered planet. We know that we need new men, but exactly what manner of new men? Can the old men be reshaped, or is it necessary to work only with the young? Is the dream of new men, so recurrent in mankind's thoughts, a chimera—an impossible dream?

We will soon learn the answer to the last question, for unless a new culture of men is rapidly evolved, there will be no men, or at least no men leading any kind of life remotely resembling that of ODC citizens today. The question of what manner of new men (or new women) we should have is much more complex. As Margaret Mead has indicated, they will represent a new stage of cultural evolution, a new set of life styles. These new life styles must transform the overdeveloped countries and permit them to de-develop. They must be spaceman life styles, having in common understanding and respect for the finite and fragile nature of our planet and the necessity for harmony among its crew.

The key to new life styles is a shift of emphasis from material to human values. We must reduce our material wants to a level which can be sustained by a stable population over a long period of time. At the same time, we must encourage the full development of creative energy drawn from our greatest natural resource—our potential as human beings. Our end must be a life of satisfaction for each individual; our means must be free self-expression of the individual compatible with the rights of all other human beings. The change will be difficult for most Americans, young and old, conditioned as we have been toward expressing ourselves through possessions. But there is abundant evidence from both within and outside of Western culture that human beings do live extremely satisfying lives with a minimum of material possessions. Intellectual activity, art, music, sexual pleasure, good food, good friends, stimulating conversation, sports, hunting, fishing and gardening are just some examples of pleasures requiring a minimum of physical trappings. Many of these, however, are denied to a substantial portion of Americans in today's affluent spectator society. Indeed, a combination of indoctrination and circumstances greatly restricts their options. Too many have been told from childhood that sexual pleasure is bad. Too few realize what good food tastes like, since so much overprocessed, non-nutritious material is carried in their local supermarkets. Crowded, smoggy cities limit the opportunities for enjoying outdoor sports, solitude, or the wonders of nature. There are, in fact, enormous intrinsic advantages and joys in simplifying our life-style.

As an ultimate goal, the culture of the new men must provide a maximum number of options to pursue one's own interests and a minimum number of assigned tasks. As we suggested earlier, this includes the rejection of our Western hangups on the Protestant ethic and compulsive labor. Many Americans suffer from guilt when they are doing something they enjoy, instead of what they "have to do." This guilt must be expunged. Dramatic changes must be made in the early teaching of our children by parents and schools. Diversity of experience and an appreciation for differences must be encouraged at every step.

A specific attitude that must change as rapidly as

possible is our national love of competition. Although competition may have been acceptable in a frontier situation where there were seemingly infinite resources, it is no longer compatible with the solutions to many of our problems. The time is here for us to cooperate with each other to solve our common problems and to provide for our real material needs. We cannot afford a competitive space race or an arms race. We no longer can afford the luxury of numerous competing brands of cars, refrigerators, washing machines and other products which differ primarily in their images rather than in effective functioning performance. It is perfectly obvious that many industries are merely maintaining the illusion of a competitive market, when a blatant oligopoly actually exists. Some individuals in our competitive society are lining their pockets at the expense of others and of the rest of the world. This kind of activity is lauded by the old men; it must be condemned by the new.

Competition between players in games is great fun, and has been used in the past as a device for preparing the young for a competitive life. The new men must understand that life can no longer be considered a competitive game. If, for instance, we continue to compete for material things we will succeed in exhausting our nonrenewable resources, bring about the complete destruction of the Earth's ecosystems, and everyone will lose. We now suspect, in addition, that the spirit of materialistic competition has extremely detrimental effects on our interpersonal relationships.

Somehow, our society must replace its present emphasis on materialism and consumerism. We must begin to concentrate on maximizing the growth of each individual spirit, rather than each individual bank account. A progressive government easily could encourage this social trend. Limiting the amount of material wealth that could be held or inherited would certainly be an incentive to give nonmaterial gifts to our children and to our friends. In a truly free society, the individual would not be imprisoned by societal conditioning that drives him to acquire, possess, and succeed, as measured solely by material standards. In our consumer-oriented society, our children are enslaved by advertisements and sales pitches in a more subtle but every bit as callous fashion as any totalitarian state that politically shapes the minds of its young.

Think about the institution known as The Christmas Season. About the middle of July, some helpful soul on the radio reminds you that there are only 117 shopping days left until Christmas. By mid-September, the spirit is really upon us—people are ordering their Christmas cards. Halloween has barely deposited its yearly blanket of candy wrappers on the lawn when the first pre-Christmas ads appear, soon followed by the tasteless Christmas decorations put up on the main street to enhance the shopping spirit. Who will ever forget those delightful, last minute shopping trips on the 23rd and 24th of December with the rest of the mob engaged in the same miserable rite? *That* is a joyous prelude to the holiday season? In spite of the standing jokes on the real meaning of green in the Christmas colors, that holiday season continues to be a veritable orgy of buying and consuming—a monument to the spiritual bankruptcy of our society.

What would happen if people were to abandon the ethic of Mammon in favor of the spirit of love and remembrance? If one felt the desire to give someone else a material gift, what a pleasant surprise it would be to receive something which had been handmade and had some of the personality and the spirit of the giver in its conception and form. Some people, especially children, already follow and enjoy this custom. Perhaps when most of us feel free to express our emotions more openly, the spirit of gathering together to celebrate a joyous occasion might supplant the need for material symbols of our feelings.

Around the end of the Second World War there was much talk about a three or four day work week, and more leisure time. But somehow we sidetracked ourselves and became confused, we grew to value things much more than ourselves. Certainly the origins of this trend are much further in the past than the 1940's; the roots go back to a time when men lived in constant physical need. But the early post-war years were the time of decision, and we chose—or were duped into—the path of ever more material goods—material wealth far beyond that necessary to nurture body or soul.

As our post-war needs were increasingly being met, it became necessary for American business to spur sales and the growth of the economy by creating new demands to replace the former needs which had been satisfied. Thus the advertising industry came to play a central role in our society. The concept of "fashion" was extended far beyond clothes and was supplemented by "planned obsolescence." Both are linked to the idea of progress as a positive value; we were led to believe that change must be good, new must be better than old. Where possible, products were designed so that they would break or wear out after a short period of time. Designs were changed rapidly and people were persuaded that it was socially unacceptable to be associated with the older merchandise. Advertising has also played a major role in foisting a vast number of seemingly diverse but actually very similar products on the public. Always the pitch is the same—a series of half-truths to persuade the consumer to switch from Tweedle-dum to Tweedle-dee. The *image* of the product is merchandized, not the product itself.

Among the new men there must therefore be new economists. They must develop a sophisticated economics of stability and find new ways of defining and evaluating utility. They must also design a system with built-in dampers of inequity. Economics must become a science in which the competition is to find ways to satisfy human needs that minimize environmental impact while maximizing human well-being. The new economists will have their hands full. For instance, a spaceman economy implys diametrically different ideas of property rights, especially those residing in land and minerals, than are currently accepted. The new economists will be charged with designing an entire new system and planning the conversion to that system. It is an economic challenge that dwarfs all that have preceded it.

Obviously, as we move to a new economics, the American way of life must change. Our struggles to compete for the dubious privilege of over-consumption wreak havoc on our bodies, our psyches and our environment. What we should be seeking as a nation is freedom and growth of the individual, rather than freedom of the market and growth of the economy.

Competition and acquisitiveness are widely believed to be genetically programed human behavior. To many individuals in Western cultures, any other form of human existence is inconceivable. They do not understand that our dilemma is an unfortunate outgrowth of a Judeo-Christian heritage, which has produced a blind science and technology and a berserk econo-centric culture (in large part shared by both capitalist and socialist societies). That many human societies have thrived without mad competition is unknown to these culture-bound people. They do not know that Eskimos built a culture based on cooperation rather than competition, one in which the idea of private property played no major role. They are unfamiliar with the Eastern and gentle Pacific cultures in which man lives (or lived) a leisurely life of harmony with nature.

The hustle, competition, materialism and consumerism of Western society is not a phenomenon springing from man's genetic nature—it is a product of cultural evolution. Other societies have taken entirely different paths. Still others have become very competitive, even hostile, but have not developed the technology that permits competitiveness to lead to the destruction of the society (although some, for instance in New Guinea, may have come very close to destroying themselves through constant warfare). Our cultural behavior, then, is not preordained by our genes: it can, at least in theory, be changed.

The flexibility of societal behavior has been demonstrated repeatedly in the past century by people as diverse as the Japanese and the Mohawk Indians. These peoples, and many others, have altered much of their own cultural background and adapted themselves very successfully to the Western way of life. Under the pressure of great need, people have demonstrated an amazing capability for changing their ways. If our society can recognize the need, it too might change.

What specific directions might such change take? Besides a trend away from competition, materialism and consumerism, there are elements in our cultural tradition that can be evoked as the struggle to find new configurations of values develops. Among these are ideals of fairness, honesty, generosity, compassion and love. We can restore these old values to a place of honor, and at the same time adopt some new ones to accompany them.

Young people today in many countries are already experimenting with new life styles, some of which might well be incorporated into the culture of the new man. Communal life, for example, might not appeal to everyone, but it certainly fosters a spirit of community and cooperation among those participating. This is particularly true of children who have been reared communally; for instance, in Israeli kibbutzim. Such a spirit of cooperation, if it can be extended to include all of humanity, will be essential if we are to solve our planetwide problems.

The rewards of marriage, indeed the institution of marriage itself, will in the future be very different from our traditional ones. Children will no longer be considered the prime reason for marriage for most people. Rather, the rewards will be sought within the relationship itself. A variety of marriage styles is already beginning to appear; they may one day be sanctioned by society as alternate forms to the traditional. One is an informal, easily dissolved marriage for the childless. Another is group marriage, which might be either formal or informal, with or without children.

Such drastic change in the forms of marriage will inevitably have profound effects on the status of women. The new women may have much to offer in restoring Spaceship Earth to equilibrium. The female approach to our problems is bound to be different from that of the male; in the interests of variety alone we have everything to gain by encouraging women to achieve positions of leadership in the new society, quite aside from the fact that they constitute more than half the population!

What place might children occupy in this society? Contrary to the accusations of those who think birth control is "anti-life," children will come to be valued more highly than they are today. One reason for this is simply that they will be fewer, and therefore more precious. It is to be hoped that unplanned, undesired children will become a thing of the past. Presumably, large families will be rare, if they exist at all. The parents of such families will be people who truly wish to devote their lives to children. Other such people might, instead, choose to be teachers or follow some other career that is involved with child welfare.

In the new society, education will be a subject of great importance. Children will learn early that their own well-being is dependent upon the well-being of all other human beings and upon the well-being of the world's ecological systems. They will also learn how to care for Spaceship Earth, to keep it running smoothly into the indefinite future. They will grow up to consider it their pleasant duty to spend at least part of their time serving as crewmen on Spaceship Earth. They will expect to participate on a regular basis in the governance and maintenance of the ship, and to spend part of their time in the service of their fellow passengers. They will also expect to continue their education throughout their lives so as to maximize the value both of their contribution to society and of their own existence.

There are, of course those who claim that most people are only fit for the role of passenger, that leadership and real contributions to society will always be the function of an elite. We disagree. There is no theoretical reason why almost all human beings cannot make strong positive contributions to society. We have never come close to exploiting the genetic potential of Homo sapiens, and it is high time that we design a society which will do so. The thesis that the "masses" are by nature docile and dumb is difficult to support in an increasingly revolutionary world. The bravery of many Soviet citizens pressing for changes in their dictatorial government, the intelligence, courage and tenacity of the Viet Cong, Biafrans, Czechs, and Cubans in the face of massive attempts at repression and the growing dissent against conformity in the United States all indicate that even in the wrong cultural milieu large numbers of people will move in the right direction.

Look at some of the small but hopeful signs in the United States. In the 1970 elections some of the candidates with the worst records on environmental issues were defeated on those issues. People know that we are in ecological trouble, and the bland, reassuring rhetoric of many politicians on this subject no longer fools them. More and more people realize that the proliferation of huge, dangerous automobiles is destroying us all—profiteers and victims alike. Crusader Ralph Nader has exposed the automobile industry in all its glory, and he shows no inclination to let the leaders of the industry scurry back into the cracks of the woodwork. Women are beginning not only to resist the dictates of the fashion industry, but to insist that they are human beings in their own right, not merely mindless automata to serve as economic objects for industry and sexual objects for men.

What is wrong with the U.S. today is especially obvious to a significant portion of the young, a group to whom, hopefully, the future belongs. If there is any hope at all for the world, it lies in the utterly unprecedented generation gap which now separates many of our young people from most of their elders. This group of young people is the leading edge of the counter-culture. They are the vanguard of Margaret Mead's prefigurative culture. In the terminology of Charles Reich,[1] they, along with some of their elders, are entering "Consciousness III." Today they are disaffected young; tomorrow, with any luck, they will be the new men.

They know what Stewart Udall is talking about when he says that "more and bigger is not necessarily better." They understand that the deaths of an American Marine from a Viet Cong booby trap and of a Vietnamese child from USAF napalm are equally tragic—and that their blood stains our hands as well as the hands of those we permit to remain in positions of power and responsibility. They know that a pile of junk from Detroit will never substitute for a loving friend in bed—that night baseball will never replace sex. They know that the President's Commission on Obscenity and Pornography should have been studying racism among our politicians, "ecological" advertisements by bigtime polluters (ecopornography), generals in search of bigger budgets, the AEC, the DOD, the A.M.A., the National Association of Manufacturers, and the Chamber of Commerce. This group of our young also understands that the massive violence we are visiting on Indochina does not justify the death of one student or janitor in a bombed campus building. They see that the residues of violence lose their toxicity slowly and that, if the new men stoop to the level of the old, then the game is lost.

Much can be said in criticism of today's young people; perhaps the most serious indictments is that the majority of them may well turn out to resemble their parents.

[1] Charles Reich, *The Greening of America* (New York: Random House, 1970).

They are "young fogies" who have bought the fairy stories of their society, hook, line and sinker. All they want to do is to grow up to grab their piece of the action. They are no more in the vanguard of desirable change than is Spiro Agnew or Leonid Brezhnev. Also absent from that vanguard are those who, disgusted with the growing hypocrisy of America or horrified at what they have seen in Vietnam, are drawn into a life of violent revolutionary acts. Some, rather politically inclined, adopt a form of violent revolutionary Marxism. They study Marx, Marcuse, Mao, Lenin, and Ché, and build a personal philosophical base from which to examine and attack the decaying society around them. Others, with less mental stamina or greater personal psychological problems, merely learn some of the radical rhetoric and become left-wing activists. The actions of these diverse groups of young people are understandable, but, in our opinion, they are counterproductive to any hope of a livable world in the future. Straight young people who accept governmental violence without protest and the revolutionary young who attempt to answer government violence in kind *both strengthen that violent government*. If we are to survive, we must weaken the corporate state, not enhance its worst attributes.

However, the great majority of disaffected young are neither Marxists nor bombers, although they tend to share many goals with them. They have had it with racism, consumerism, poverty-in-the-midst-of-plenty, and the warfare state. They want the system bent at least to the point where its ideals and realities bear some relation to each other. And they share with many of us who are no longer young great despair as to whether it is possible. Consider these quotes from readers of *Natural History Magazine,* hardly a revolutionary journal.

> "I personally do not think the environment can be saved. Man in my opinion, is too egocentric to pay the price in time . . ."

". . . my 30-year commitment to a cleaner, better, happier world was a hopeless dream."

"I personally believe it is time for man to leave the earth; he is more of a destroyer than a builder. Let earth renew itself."

"I have a sense life is over . . ."

"I shout at slobs that I catch littering and polluting (I'd shoot them if it were legal)."

"I keep dreaming of bombing Con Ed."

"We are totally pessimistic for the long range."

"I do not think man is going to make it."

". . . there is no cure for human misery or inequity as long as overpopulation exists."

"Am moving to New Guinea in October."

". . . gave up in despair and am moving to Australia."

"I pray a lot for the world."

"No telling how long any of us will be here."

The hope that is contained in all this despair is that an understanding of the need for new men and new life styles is spreading rapidly. More and more people are realizing that the mere treatment of the symptoms of our disease will no longer suffice; fundamental changes will be required if we are to have a chance.

Does this mean that all Americans must eschew capitalism, grow long hair, smoke pot, and live off the land in communes? A strong trend in that direction at present would lead to a breakdown of society and the death of most of its numbers. We live in an extremely complex technological culture which is utterly dependent for continuance in its present form on believers in the Protestant ethic, profit-oriented economists and businessmen, and warmongers. If they were all instantly reformed, the lights would go out and almost everyone would starve to death. The system as it is now constructed requires "old men" to run it. It can be changed, but it will take time and planning. The first order of business is to change the direction of the industrial juggernaut, not to dismantle it. A large scale "back to nature" movement at this time would be fatal. We must keep the trains and trucks running, if only because trains and trucks transport food and other necessities. Until the world can be reshaped and its population drastically reduced, we are stuck with mechanized agriculture and highly efficient transportation. That is, as long as we want to survive, and as long as we want to be able to help our less fortunate fellow men in the UDCs, we must take advantage of our highly developed technology. We must break and tame the technological monster and then use it as the progenitor of a humane future technology. The system cannot be changed overnight.

The new men must come through gentle conversion and natural replacement. Certainly the antisocial activities of the old men and technology will have to be quickly stopped, but this should be done with a maximum of subtlety. There is no point in waving a red flag in front of the bulls. If the new men in the United States demand a replacement of capitalism with "socialism" (or "Marxism" or "communism"), the old will recoil in horror. They, for the most part, have not the vaguest notion what either capitalism or socialism is all about. They have, however, been indoctrinated to react negatively to the words "socialism" and "communism" as reflexively as Pavlov's dogs were taught to salivate at the ringing of a bell. A crusade for less state control, more freedom of speech, or limited capitalism from new men in the Soviet Union would elicit a similar over-reaction there. The new men must work toward a stable world economy; an end to starvation, exploitation and oppression; more equitable distribution of income and power within and between nations; more individual freedom of speech and thought everywhere; but never toward specific "isms."

In short, new men must have the sense to minimize conflict with the old. They must remember that, while they get their sexual kicks out of sex, others get theirs from anti-smut crusades. The new men must understand that a society already hooked on revenue-producing alcohol and nicotine, as well as a vast assortment of other dangerous drugs, is naturally disturbed by the upsurge of the use of marijuana. After all, it seems to produce more pleasure than the others and may even be less harmful (it seems unlikely that it, or any other drug, can ever be declared "completely harmless").

Nothing distresses the victims of the Protestant ethic more than the thought of people leading a less hateful life than they lead. The most vituperative letters received by advocates of population control tend to come from repressed mothers of large families. They obviously have hated their role, but did their "duty." Now someone tells them that not only could they have led different, more fulfilling lives, but also that their "duty" was a disservice to humanity. Who can blame them for being enraged! Rather than rub people's noses in their own messes, we should encourage them to join the new men in new pleasures and rewards to whatever extent they wish—and make them feel welcome.

There is no reason to believe that, if a full-fledged culture of new men does evolve, all of them (or even most) necessarily will in any way resemble the more "hip" of today's young. We suspect, indeed we hope, that considerable diversity in attitudes and life styles will exist within an ecologically sane culture. We hope that, while some people will "do their thing" by cultivating the land, others will find fulfillment as scientists, businessmen, social workers, teachers, artists, clerks, politicians, physicians, medieval historians, and what-have-you. The operative word is "fulfillment." The goals of society must center on each individual's leading the life he or she wishes to lead, while also insuring that society functions well and that its collective goals are met. Those who claim society will not be able to function if this occurs may be right (although those who so argue are inevitably doing *their* own thing—it is always someone else who must accept the inevitable drudgery). It is still a goal worth striving for. With a small population size and a technology designed to maximize human happiness rather than the profits of a few—a technology subordinate to man rather than vice-versa—the game might be won.

We are the first to admit that our vision is utopian; a world in which new men live in harmony with their environment and their fellow men; a world in which a diversity of ideas, skin colors, cultures, and personalities is one of the most treasured values; a world in which compassion for other living creatures, quite likely our only companions in the solar system, is universal; a world in which work, as a *chore,* is infrequent or unknown; a world in which those who develop and tend the technology that *serves* man will be happy in the knowledge that they are doing a creative and important job—just as creative as that done by an artist or a linguist.

Impossible? Perhaps. The new men will be opposed by all those with social myopia and a vested interest in the status quo. They will be opposed with sneers, talk of silly idealism or "lack of political feasibility." They will be opposed by all those who have never considered how infeasible it will be to have almost everybody dead. For, as we have said, the choice is basically new men or no men.

It is very easy to fall into a pit of hopeless pessimism as one considers the steady deterioration of Spaceship Earth. But one finds occasionally some small signs that the trend may be reversed, that the new men may, with compassion, courage and foresight, save us yet. There are times when it seems as though they might; when men choose exile rather than serve an imperialist army or when the young no longer accept the puerile speeches of run-of-the-mill politicians. Those and similar portents must give us the will to make our stand. The young chaplain of the University of the Pacific, Larry Meredith, said it well in his benediction to a conservative audience at the University's 1970 Convocation for granting of degrees:

Let this be our benediction:

Let us stand here in contrition and commitment,
    those who will labor for peace,
who will support population control and humane
    abortion laws,
who will support the right of farm workers to un-
    ionize,
who would abolish nuclear weapons and protect
    the right to political dissent,
who believe financially in participatory education,
who still feel horror and shame over our national
    sickness, our imperial mentality—a malaise
    which has divided our country, wounded and
    killed our students, polarized our races, and
    threatened the good earth with apocalypse.

Let this be our benediction:

for Zion's sake we will not keep silent,
for Jerusalem's sake we will not rest,
    until our swords are plowshares,
    our spears pruning hooks,
    and our nations learn war no more.

Appendices

Appendix

Tactics for First Class Passengers

WHAT SPECIFICALLY CAN average First Class Passengers do now to change the course of their country and pave the way for the emergence of new men, new values, a new culture? The answer is, of course, that they must reclaim some of the power which has been gradually taken from them and vested in the corporate state. There is some debate at the moment about the exact nature of that state and precisely who holds how much power within it, but there is little dispute about the really crucial points. Power in the United States is almost as concentrated as wealth. As measured both by who makes the decisions and who benefits, very few people run the United States.

Whether the decision makers are mostly the extremely rich and those they own and control or whether they include sizable numbers of more

[1] Those interested in this debate are referred to the stimulating books by Domhoff and Ballard, Galbraith, Hacker, Kolko and Lundberg, listed in the bibliography.

or less independent managers and technicians need not concern us here.[1] At the moment, decisions are not made in any real sense by the people of the United States or by individuals who represent the best interests of the people at large. What is worse, the corporate state acts like a dinosaur rushing toward an abyss, too stupid or with too much momentum to turn aside. To put it another way, whoever is making the decisions is doing a very bad job.

What strategy is available, then, to divert the dinosaur before it takes us over the edge? The revolutionary or radical answer is to shoot it or blow it up. Only 3.5 per cent of current college youth is categorised as revolutionary.[2] The liberal answer is to use the channels provided by the system to change the system.

The radical answer suffers from a great defect. It is difficult to stop a charging dinosaur with a BB gun or a firecracker, and, relative to the power of the corporate state, that is all the radicals have. The defect of the liberal answer is even greater. It has been tried, and it hasn't worked—you cannot stop a charging dinosaur by whispering in its ear, either.

We would like to suggest a multivalent approach to solving the problem, but first we would like to make one point crystal clear. There is no a priori reason why the dinosaur should *not* go over the edge. Contrary to widely-held American beliefs, everything does not always come out all right in the end. Individuals have difficulty imagining their own extinction; so do societies and species. We offer no sure solution, only directions in which to try.

[2] Richard M. Scammon and Ben J. Wattenberg, *The Real Majority* (New York: Coward-McCann, Inc., 1970), p. 52. See the rest of Chapter 4 for further documentation.

Fundamentally, our approach is to use grass-roots power. We have an elitist society with decisions in the hands of a few, and it is not working. We make no assumption that a more broadly based governmental structure automatically will lead to more intelligent decisions (although it could hardly avoid leading to greater equity). But we see no other choice except to try that route. We also see no choice but to attempt to wrest power from the special interests without destroying the technological apparatus of the nation. For, as we have indicated earlier, that apparatus is necessary if we are to save the world.

Charles Reich argues[3] that a fight to gain power is unnecessary, that all we have to do is await the emergence of the new men, of his "Consciousness III." He states:

"There is a great discovery awaiting those who choose a new set of values—a discovery comparable to the revelation that the Wizard of Oz was just a humbug. The discovery is simply this: there is nobody whatever on the other side. Nobody wants inadequate housing and medical care-only the machine. Nobody wants war except the machine. And even businessmen, once liberated, would like to roll in the grass and be in the sun. There is no need, then, to fight any group of people. They are all fellow sufferers. There is no reason to fight the machine. It can be made the servant of man. Consciousness III can make a new society." [4]

Reich might well be right; if we had the time, the new men might gradually take over and all would be well. But we haven't got a generation—we only have a few years. And the people in power are, perhaps with the best of intentions,

[3] Charles Reich, *The Greening of America* (New York: Random House, 1970), Chapter 11.
[4] Reich, p. 348.

killing us all. Here is what James D. Reilly, a Vice President of Consolidated Coal Company, said in a speech at Pittsburgh on May 8, 1969:

"The conservationists who want strip miners to restore land are stupid idiots, Socialists, and Commies who don't know what they are talking about. I think it is our bounden duty to knock them down and subject them to the ridicule they deserve." [5]

If James Reilly is not an enemy, he will do until one comes along. Our society is loaded with enemies, and we cannot merely wait for them to die off. And we cannot, as Reich suggests, hole up until the bad times are over. The bad times will probably kill us in our holes, and if they don't, they may well outlast us.

There is nothing extreme about our programme for changing the direction of the corporate beast. Basically, we suggest that public education and consumer boycott should lay the groundwork for political action.

A number of things give us hope. The first is that survival itself is the issue. Once people understand that, they will fight like hell for it—even the Mr. Reillys of the world. Many of the people with power are smart, some are liberal, and all want to survive. When *they* can be convinced that our current course is killing *them,* the course will be changed. The second hopeful thing is that it is becoming more and more difficult to avoid the truth. The situation is deteriorating on all sides, and the need for fundamental change is becoming increasingly apparent. The third reason for hope is the appearance of some new men, the development of Reich's New Consciousness, especially among some of our young. If these new

[5] Quoted by Harry M. Caudill in "Are Conservation and Capitalism Compatible?" in H. W. Helfrich, Jr., *Agenda for Survival; The Environmental Crisis—2* (New Haven: Yale University Press, 1970), p. 177.

men turn outward to help their fellow men, they may be a powerful engine for change.

Consumer Power

We need grassroots power, and one way to grassroots power is through a consumer movement. In the U.S. Ralph Nader's Center for the Study of Responsive Law and John Banzhaf's group at the School of Law of George Washington University in Washington, D.C. are both doing good jobs in the area of legal reform of consumer protection legislation. Consumer's Union, through their house publication, *Consumer's Report,* is doing a fine job of educating the consumer on which products are the best buy, but it does not advocate group action, nor does it of course suggest that purchasing be restricted in any way. Progress in this area is greatly impeded by the vested interests that wield multi-billion dollar influence in our government. The last thing they want to see is effectively organized consumer power. We already know that we must neutralize the influence of these special interest lobbies in some way—the question is "how?"

The answer would seem to lie in organizing a *national cooperative movement* which will exercise great economic and political power. A buyers' cooperative committed to the realistic use of economic power could reorganize American and other business practices by boycotting and striking on a mass scale. It could pledge a fixed percentage of its sales income to supporting political action population-environment groups. Hopefully, it could form the basis for a mass movement. Not only will the consumer pay reduced prices for ecologically sound products, but also he will be indirectly supporting the population-environment groups which can really *do* something about changing our political institutions.

With the support of groups like Nader's Raiders, a truly national, powerful Consumer's Union could force the American business community to exercise social responsibility toward their customers. The rationale is simple: *everyone* is a consumer—even the poorest individual is a consumer at least of food and housing. Labour has long been organised, but no one has proceeded systematically to organise the hundreds of billions of dollars of consumer purchasing power. Consumers must have a say in the production of the goods which are offered for sale if our society is to survive.

Can you imagine the impact if a national cooperative were to say, "For the next two years we are not going to buy groceries at Safeway or automotive products from General Motors!" Obviously, this threat would be lifted if the corporation involved, whatever it might be, met some predetermined, specific performance requirements, such as buying only union-grown food; not selling products that come in nonbiodegradable wrappings or no deposit, no-return containers; reducing the prices on certain items or not selling them at all; ceasing to produce major cosmetic automobile model changes year after year without much improvement of safety features; making more durable, smaller, less powerful, and recyclable vehicles; reducing the prices of automotive products. If the boycotts were successful, the consumers' cooperative obviously would have to help support the workers unemployed because of boycotts by giving them additional food discounts and contributing to strike funds. But, hopefully, the large scale and impact of the boycotts would make them short-term affairs.

There are enough other places to buy goods in this country so that corporate giants who refuse to participate in a competitive economy can be heavily penalised. Oligopolistic capitalism in this country has had its day; now it is time for the enforced consumer to become a user by choice.

The same sort of tactics may be applied to the housing situation. Tenants' unions and strikes, if well organized and financially underwritten by consumer groups, could be extremely effective. The key to the entire strategy is organisation and solidarity, just as it was in the labour union movement.

Once consumers have been organised, very potent political weapons will reside in their confidence and economic power. Imagine what would happen if, say, two million taxpayers deducted 60 per cent from their federal taxes, an amount proportional to their share of the military budget. Such massive group action would be a far different problem for the military-industrial complex than the scattered refusal to pay war taxes by such courageous individuals as Joan Baez. Most citizens do not like paying taxes anyway, so it might not take much to convince a large number of average taxpayers to withhold a sizable chunk of their taxes, especially when they knew that many other people were doing the same thing. Even if the taxpayers ultimately yielded to the pressure of governmental lawsuits and agreed to pay their taxes, the backlog of paperwork and the delay in receiving the taxes would cause financial havoc for the government programs. If the government tried to hold on welfare, social security, or other popular disbursements in order to continue supporting the military, then people would really *feel* where their money was being spent.

Once a cooperative movement had gained momentum, it could also engage in an enormous campaign to re-educate other consumers and to change their buying habits. The pitch might be: "Try to live below your means! It will be good for your family's economic situation, and it may also help to save the world." Not only would people be urged to buy less, but to buy better quality products, whenever there was a choice they could afford. They might also be asked to change their dietary habits for their own good health and for the health of the world-wide eco-system. Much of the food sold to the American public in supermarkets is nutritionally substandard. Recent reports on breakfast cereals, bread that has most of the important nutrients removed, and on the receptive practices used to treat meat to make it look fresher give some indication of the degree of responsibility that the food industry feels toward its captive clientele. It is extremely difficult for an American to eat an adequately balanced diet, especially without taking in too many calories. Many food additives are of doubtful safety, and the highly saturated fats produced in our higher-yield meat industry may be extremely dangerous to health. An effective national consumer group could drive America's "plastic bread" and all of its sleazy relatives from the grocer's shelves.

Giant corporations must be shown that there is extreme public disapproval of their activities. Suggested tactics have ranged from shutting down industry switchboards through organized telephone campaigns to long term boycotts of one or more automobile manufacturer's products. Certainly, it would be no hardship for everyone who needed an automobile during the year to purchase a used car. But one must also weigh the effects of such a boycott on the employees of the automobile industry. It is encumbent, therefore, on boycotting organisations to include programmes in their planning to alleviate the distress which may be experienced by some segments of the labour force.

We do not wish to denigrate the individual symbolic protest tactics suggested in *The Environmental Hand-book* and *Ecotactics* or the efforts of environmental groups such as Ecology Action. But they must be recognised for exactly what they are—symbolic protests. As we have indicated, changing individual attitudes and patterns of behaviour as expressed through personal life styles is extremely important. But the larger institutions which limit the alternatives for individual behaviour must also be changed before any really significant progress in solving the population-environment crisis can be made. And, before these basic institutions can be changed, we must gain the power to change them. This, of course, means gaining control of the political system.

A prerequisite, if this overall strategy is to have any chance of success, is to enlist more people into the survival movement as soon as possible. A prime target should be the recruitment of the young. They must be reached before they fossilise into standard American consumers and polluters. Those of us who are over thirty must try to infiltrate the education process by teaching, participating in the parent-teacher associations, or by becoming involved with youth in other ways. You might, for instance, be able to help young people organise programmes and ecology fairs by finding informed speakers for such meetings, or, even better, by becoming well-informed and speaking yourself.

Concerned people who are fortunate enough to be young can also contribute. If you are a school or college student, there are two effective tactics you can employ: talk to your parents and their friends, and bring social pressure to bear on your own friends and acquaintances whose attitudes are contrary to environmental principles or who exhibit ecologically unsound behaviour. Surprising as it may seem, parents are listening to their children more and more.

Keep after your parents. Show your concern by becoming a walking encyclopedia on population and environment. Give them books to read. Start out with popular, straightforward books, such as *Moment in the Sun* and *The Rich and the Super-Rich*. Discuss the issues with them; tell them about the candidates who are strong on population-environment issues and discourage them from voting for old-style politicians who do not understand the urgency of the crisis. You will have maximum impact on your parents and their friends if you are well informed, stick to the issues, and remain patient and unemotional.

The same procedures hold true for friends of your own age. The only difference is that you should make it clear that certain attitudes and behaviour are socially unacceptable. If one of your classmates expresses a desire to have more than two natural children, inform him of the facts and make sure that he understands the seriousness of the situation. If one of your friends wants a big new car or buys lots of new clothes to keep up with the new fashions, let him know that his attitudes are not only ecologically destructive, but repugnant to you. If one of your friends stops riding a bicycle to school or work and begins driving a car, let him know that you disapprove; or if he stops driving a car and starts riding a bicycle, let him know how pleased you are. You will be surprised how much impact the opinion of peers can have. Adults may have similar effects on their associates, although the older one is, the more thoroughly entrenched consumerism and other attitudes are likely to be.

These are just a few suggestions, but whatever you do (unless you are already active in a national organisation), start out on a local level and work within the institutions most familiar to you. These are the places where you will be most effective and where you can exert your maximum influence. Young or old, if you are a member of any church, youth or community group, etc., work within your own organisation to steer its activities and policies in the direction of survival. Almost everyone belongs to at least one organisation at school, at work, or in connection with sports, hobbies, church, social activities, etc. If you are not affiliated with some such group, join one and make your views known. Even if you do not completely convince anyone, at least you may expose others to your ideas and to the issues involved.

Besides attacking on the local front, you may well want to participate in the larger battle. There are several national action organisations concerned with population-environmental issues with which you can affiliate. Most will give you assistance if you want to start a new chapter (see Appendix III). At the present time, the formation of new national groups will only tend to divide the population-environment movement, and unity is going to be essential in the long, hard fight to come. We receive a great many letters describing groups that have just been formed and who are now soliciting financial assistance and public support. Although it is encouraging that so many people are interested, more consolidated effort is needed in order to apply a maximum amount of pressure on specific targets. Once some tangible victories have been chalked up, there will be more public support for a broader approach.

The very real danger of being divided and dissipating energy was apparent at the First National

Congress on Optimum Population and Environment held in Chicago in June, 1970. Unfortunately, much of the energy generated there by the 1200 delegates, representing hundreds of groups, was expressed as schisms between factions. Much time and effort was spent trying to achieve unity, instead of being directed outward toward common objectives. "Divide and conquer" is a time-honoured defensive tactic that many special interest groups will be quick to employ against us.

Once you have affiliated with an organisation, pick a specific local project and get going. You may wish to support a "good guy" in a political race, boycott a polluter, or picket a hospital which will not perform legal abortions or sterilisations on demand. Remember, you can have the most impact on those issues which you and other members of your group know best. Remember also that time is short, and therefore political action should have top priority whenever possible.

Political Power

A great weakness of our major political parties is that we never hear from them except during election years, and, even then, only when they want something. A sustained campaign must be launched to inform large numbers of citizens of the issues and to keep these concerns in the forefront of their minds. In other words, we face the unenviable task of trying to educate and politicize millions of ordinarily apathetic citizens. But we have the best of circumstances under which to do so. The deteriorating environment will not go away. Its problems will thrust themselves on a public trained to feel entitled to the "best," until that public begins to ask *why*. It is only a question of time. The sooner we can get the question asked, the better. The short-term goal is to elect ecologically-oriented leaders for our ODCs, and to effect great personnel changes in state and local governments. This means working to elect public officials at all levels who understand the urgency of the population-environment crisis and who are willing dramatically to modify the old system in a last ditch attempt to find solutions. Not only must we defeat the pseudo-environmentalists and do-nothing candidates, we must sustain our efforts until we have removed most of those presently in power from the system and modified it structurally, so that a similar anti-human juggernaut cannot evolve again. The only hope of success lies in organisation and persistence.

Organisation and persistence could provide the United States with an alternative to the business as usual, Democratic/Republican party brand of politics. People who are sincerely interested in population-resource-environment issues should be offered something new and effective for a change. We think that the emergence of a new major political party may be necessary. Reluctantly, we have come to the conclusion that the two major political parties, left on their own, are unlikely to give us any alternatives. There is simply too much inertia in the ranks of the old-style politicians. Even if we could convince the parties in power to adopt strong population-environment planks in their platforms, the candidates would adhere to the old politics and continue, once elected, to permit the government to be run by well-financed business interests. So powerful are these interests—the power lobby, the automobile-highway lobby, the oil lobby, the drug lobby, the food lobby, and so on—that it would be difficult for the new men to counter them, impossible for the old.

An alternative might be provided by a mobilization of grassroots power. In the U.S. it might be possible to unite all the dissatisfied liberal elements of both parties—intellectuals, minority groups, students, and those workers who have come to understand that for them there is no difference between the present Democratic and Republican parties—with any radicals willing to try coalition politics. A coalition might be formed of moderate and liberal Democrats and Republicans, and those to the left and to the right of them who have a stronger interest in survival than in perpetuating over-consumption. Organizations such as *Zero Population Growth* and *Friends of the Earth* might form the nucleus of such a coalition.

Perhaps the most optimistic scenario is one in which the new coalition takes over the Democratic Party—making it, in essence, a new party. The Republican Party resulted fundamentally from a single-issue controversy, the debate over the abolition of slavery in the 1850's. The new Democratic Party would concentrate on the single issue of survival. The strength and power of this new party would be to offer alternative candidates, policies, and political styles which neither party in its present form is willing to consider. A coalition victory under the flag of the New Democrats in 1972 could presage the absorption of liberal Republicans into that new party, and a switch of conservative Democrats into the Republican Party. That party could then provide a constructively conservative opposition.

Above all, many more First Class Passengers must become deeply involved in politics. In a democracy, the electorate gets only what it deserves and what it is willing to pay for. Expectation sets the limits on realisation, and our political system functions no better than we expect it to. As long as many of the First Class Passengers continue to shun politics as a "dirty business," their political systems will continue to be exactly that. Both the system and the politicians will rarely rise above the mediocre. Unless the electorate shouts out its disapproval and backs it up with a sustained effort and financial support, the voters will continue to get the same plastic bread and technological circuses which have been their fare for the past two decades.

There is, of course, great inertia in the American political system. Student activists, young radicals and others who have the idealism to want to change the system, must show the staying power needed to topple the vested interests of the so-called establishment. The incumbents and the special interest groups, who *do* have the perseverence and the financial backing, have long ago lost their idealism. With a combination of idealism and persistence it may be possible to effect positive changes in the system.

Two illustrations of this political reality could be seen in Earth Day and the campus strikes following the American invasion of Cambodia in the spring of 1970. A frenzy of activity and publicity about ecology culminated on April 22nd, Earth Day. After that date, numerous fair-weather "ecologists" got off the bandwagon and presumably went in search of a new fad. But a determined group persisted and helped to defeat a series of environmentally irresponsible candidates in the November 1970 elections. In contrast, the student strikes following the invasion of Cambodia were white hot, and the heat was short-lived. Two weeks after the initial protest, everything was back to "business as usual" on many campuses. The administration was effectively able to defuse the Indochina war issue because not enough people were able to apply continuous political pressure.

The environmental battles were often won in close races where conservation votes made the difference; few hawk-dove races were close enough for peace votes to turn the tide. But one should not despair over this result. Intensive political activity by peace groups since 1965 has led to the deposing of one president and an immense change in American public opinion at all levels. We must finish the job on the war and move on to attacking the disease of which it is a symbol.

If the present political system is to be revised and a new politics introduced, we must employ political judo. In other words, the momentum and mechanisms within the system must be used against the system. Finesse, rather than force, must be used in order to gain control of the system before it can be changed. This does not mean that power politics and high pressure political tactics will not be employed. On the contrary, nonviolent power must be brought to bear on the politicians and institutions that have used similar force to the public disadvantage in the past.

Organisational Detail

Although there is no single way to organise citizens' action groups and each community has its own political personality, there are several basic guidelines to follow in order to avoid the usual pitfalls into which inexperienced organisers can stray. Start small and build a good, solid, hardcore nucleus of reliable leaders before trying to go community-wide. Most organisations function because of the labours of a very few people. Do not allow a chapter to become cumbersomely large; not beyond 50 or so active members who know one another. When such a size is reached, having sister organisations or chapters working independently, although in communication, is more efficient. Strengthen your communications system by designing a "telephone tree" in which one call generates two more calls, etc. This is important to promote fast action and a short response time, both of which are absolutely critical to succeed at the legislative lobbying game.

The same principle holds true for mailings: make sure you have *complete* information on each member of your group—this includes both home and business phone numbers and addresses. If possible, it is best to standardise this information by putting it on duplicate 3″ x 5″ cards and *cross-filing* them alphabetically and also by chapter location or function in the organisation. Keep an alphabetised master sheet listing all members for quick reference; this should be updated at regular intervals. Too many organisations have collapsed unnecessarily; not from lack of energy, work, or enthusiasm, but rather, because of a poorly organised administrative section. These procedures are really simple to execute and they pay off handsomely in the end, especially under high-pressure crisis situations.

Finances, have also been the downfall of a number of groups and clubs—not merely a lack of funds to support worthwhile programs, but mismanagement of the financial affairs of the organisation. Above all else, avoid becoming overextended. Do not commit the organisation to long-range projects for which you do not have sufficient funding guaranteed. Being aggressive with your present resources is one thing; being overambitious is quite another. As soon as possible, once the organisation is large enough to justify it, get hold of a volunteer bookkeeper and accountant and for your organisation. If you cannot locate a volunteer, it is false economy not to retain the services of professionals, because in the long they will save you more in headaches and money than you will pay out in fees. Fund raising also benefits from professional advice. Subscriptions, proceeds from sales, fairs, etc., have their place, but concerted and systematic attempts to raise money from donors may make the difference between a viable and a moribund organisation.

We would like to reiterate that many problems can be avoided by working through the national organisation, which can probably give you guidance. Remember also that great care is usually necessary to avoid internal dissension in volunteer organisations. People are not necessarily compatible merely because they share a common cause. If the world is to be saved, it will be saved by the cooperation of people who agree 50 to 60 per cent of the time; 100 per cent agreement is rare indeed!

A Last Word

Although we have referred to it several times before, we would like to conclude with a reassertion of our conviction that the population-environment movement is absolutely inseparable from the antiwar movement, the drive for urban rehabilitation, prison reform, and—most importantly—the civil rights movement. The destruction of our environment is tied up to a critical extent with our prevalent philosophy of racism and the exploitation of minority groups, whether they be black, brown, yellow, red, poor, hip, or female. Any attempt to clean the air or water for white, middle-class suburbanites, or to preserve free-running streams or open spaces for the esthetic pleasure of an economic elite which can afford to use them is doomed to failure if the educational and socio-economic needs of a large, oppressed minority of people in this country are not met at the same time. There is simply no earthly reason for any ghetto dweller to pay taxes or to stand patiently by while the rest of the society seizes the "ecology cop-out" as an excuse for further delay on long overdue social, economic, and educational reforms for the deprived minority.

By the same token, the minorities who are justifiably fighting for their rights must appreciate the necessity of restoring the capacity of our bio-sphere to support life on a long-term basis. It is understandable that when confronted with a choice between laying claim to his own civil rights as a human being and working wholeheartedly for the ecology movement, a member of a mino-rity group must choose the former. But the very quality of humanity which should entitle him to be treated as a human being also obligates him, if not to support, at least not to obstruct the honest efforts of others to work on his behalf to guarantee all of us a place to exercise our equal rights as human beings.

In the long run, it is the sum total of the actions of millions of individuals that constitutes effective group action, cultural reformation, or revolution. What has become the population-environment movement began a long time ago with the indi-vidual efforts of a few. Even if you are not com-mitted to the long-term survival of the human race or to the short-term survival of your neighbour, it is in your own self-interest to consider your own survival and that of your family. If for no reason other than that of self-interest, commit yourself to act. The next time someone asks you,

"What can I do?" — tell him to slow down, live more simply by consuming less, support *Zero Population Growth* and *Friends of the Earth*, and get involved in the political process. Then *do it*. Otherwise, we shall all eventually find ourselves stranded in space on a dead Spaceship Earth with no place to go and no way to get there.

Appendix II

Population Growth and Environmental Deterioration

by Paul R. Ehrlich and John P. Holdren[1]

IN AN AGRICULTURAL or a technological society, each human individual has a negative impact on his or her environment. He is responsible for some of the simplification and resulting destabilisation of ecological systems which result from the practice of agriculture. He also participates in the utilisation of both renewable and nonrenewable resources. The total negative impact of such a society on the environment is, in the simplest terms, the products of the number of people and some measure of the per capita impact.

A great deal of complexity is, however, subsumed in that simple model. Naive observers often assume that population size and per capita impact

[1] Lawrence Radiation Laboratory, Livermore, California. This appendix is based on testimony given before the *President's Commission on Population Growth and the American Future*, November, 1970.

are independent variables, when of course they are not. For instance, Ansley Coale, in a recent article in the journal *Science,* attempted to minimise the role of population growth in environmental problems by arguing that since 1940 "Population has increased by 50 percent but per capita use of electricity has been multiplied several times." But in an overpopulated nation like the United States, per capita power use is a partial function of the number of people.

The easiest way of seeing this is to consider another simplified model. Assume that each person has links with every other person—roads, cars to drive on the roads, telephone lines, and so forth. Two people are connected by one link $(A \leftrightarrow B)$, but there are three links among three people $(A \leftrightarrow B, A \leftrightarrow C, B \leftrightarrow C)$, six links among four people $(A \leftrightarrow B, A \leftrightarrow C, A \leftrightarrow D, B \leftrightarrow C, B \leftrightarrow D, C \leftrightarrow D)$, ten links among five people, and so forth. These links involve power in their construction and use. Since the number of links increases much more rapidly than the number of people,[2] so does per capita power consumption, as a direct result of population growth.

This general phenomenon does not, however, provide the only connection between population growth and per capita power consumption. More and more people require more and more nonrenewable resources—minerals, water (which is effectively nonrenewable in many circumstances), fossil fuels, etc.—even if their per capita consumption remains the same. As the richest supplies of these resources and those nearest to centres of use are consumed, we are obliged to use lower

[2] If N is the number of people, then the number of links is $L = N(N - 1)/2$, and the number of links per capita is $(N - 1)/2$. The obvious oversimplification in this model does not destroy its basic validity.

grade ores, drill deeper, and extend our supply networks. All of these activities increase our per capita energy use.

Even food is, in part, a nonrenewable resource in our present circumstances. As the population grows, attenpts are made both to overproduce on land already farmed and to extend agriculture to marginal land. The former requires disproportionate energy use in obtaining and distributing water, fertiliser and pesticides. The latter also increases per capita energy use, since the amount of energy invested per unit yield increases as less desirable land is cultivated. Both "consume" the fertility built into the natural soil structure. Similarly, as the richest fisheries' stocks are depleted, the yield per unit effort drops, and more and more energy per capita is required to maintain the supply.[3] Once a stock is depleted it may never recover—it may be nonrenewable.

For many reasons, then, there is inevitable increase in per capita power usage accompanying population growth in any technological society which, like the United States, has largely exhausted its opportunities for economies of scale. But there are many other reasons why increasing the population of such a society often causes a disproportionate increase in environmental deterioration. One, of course, involves threshold effects. Below a certain level of pollution, trees will survive in smog. But when a small increment in population produces a small increment in smog, living trees may become dead trees. Five hundred people may be able to live around a lake and

[3] A most dramatic example of this is found in Dr. Roger Payne's 1968 analysis of the whale fisheries, summarized in Ehrlich and Ehrlich, *Population, resources, Environment* (San Francisco: W. H. Freeman, 1970).

dump their raw sewage into the lake, and the natural systems of the lake will be able to break down the sewage and keep the lake from undergoing rapid ecological change. But five hundred and five people may overload the system and result in a polluted or eutrophic lake.

Synergisms may also lead to disproportionate environmental deterioration relative to population growth. For instance, as cities push out into farmland, air pollution increasingly becomes a mixture of agricultural chemicals with power plant and automobile effluents. Sulphur dioxide from the city paralyses the cleaning mechanisms of the lungs, thus increasing the residence time in the lungs of potential carcinogens from the agricultural chemicals. The joint effect may be much greater than the sum of the individual effects.

Not only is there a connection between population size and per capita damage to the environment, but the cost of maintaining environmental quality at a given level escalates disproportionately as population size increases. This effect occurs in part because costs increase very rapidly as one tries to reduce contaminants per unit volume of effluent to lower and lower levels. Consider municipal sewage, for example. The cost of removing 80 to 90 per cent of the biochemical and chemical oxygen demand, 90 per cent of the suspended solids, and 60 per cent of the resistant organic material by means of secondary treatment is about 8 cents per thousand gallons in a large plant. But if the volume of sewage is such that its nutrient content creates a serious eutrophication problem (as is the case in the U. S. today), or if supply considerations dictate the reuse of sewage water for industry, agriculture, or groundwater recharge, then advanced treatment is necessary. The cost ranges from two to four times as much as for secondary treatment (17 cents/1000 gal.

for carbon adsorption, 34 cents/1000 gal. for disinfection to yield potable supply).[4] This dramatic example of diminishing returns in pollution control could be repeated for stack gases, automobile exhausts, and so forth.

Now consider a situation in which the limited capacity of the environment to absorb abuse requires that we hold man's impact in some sector constant as population doubles. This means per capita *effectiveness* of pollution control in this sector must double. Even without diminishing returns, per capita costs will double, yielding quadrupled total costs (and probably energy consumption) in this sector for a doubling of population. When diminishing returns or threshold effects are operative, we may easily have eightfold control costs for a doubling of population. Such arguments leave little ground for the popular assumption that a one per cent rate of population growth spawns only one per cent effects.

It is to be emphasised that "economies of scale" do not invalidate these arguments. Such savings, if available at all, would apply in the case of our example to a change in the amount of effluent to be handled at a given installation. For most technologies, the U. S. is already more than populous enough to achieve these economies and is doing so. They are accounted for in our example by citing figures for the largest treatment plants. Population growth, on the other hand, forces us into quantitative *and* qualitative changes in how we handle each unit volume of effluent—what fraction and what kinds of material we remove. Here economies of scale do not apply at all and diminishing returns are the rule.

[4] All the numbers in this paragraph are from *Cleaning Our Environment: The Chemical Basis for Action* (Washington, D.C.: The American Chemical Society, 1969), pp. 95-162.

Appendix III

Politically-Oriented Action Organisations

In the U.S. there has been a considerable growth recently of action-oriented environmental groups, both local and national. These include such organisations as Environment Action Inc., Zero Population Growth and Friends of the Earth. These new groups have emerged not only because the situation has needed much more urgent and radical action, but also because of the legal and tax restrictions which were imposed on the more traditional conservation organisations.

In the U.K. there is also a need for new organisations uncompromising in their defence of the environment, and uninhibited in the action they are prepared to take. Friends of the Earth Ltd. is one of them.

FOE is an international non-profit making organisation prepared to take aggressive legal and political action to ensure a better environment for everyone. In the U.K. it is formed as a company limited by guarantee so as to fight freely and quickly.

FOE places emphasis on practical action and recognises the need for many new organisations to share the work. It is also aware of the need to give more help to existing conservation groups which have been labouring long and hard. Our Earth is threatened and needs every friend it has.

FOE intends firstly to pursue an active publishing programme with Ballantine Books, to provide the best possible information about the remedial action required to meet current threats to the environment. It also intends to encourage further research aimed at a greater understanding of the impact on the Earth of Man, and his technological society.

Unhampered by any party-political allegiance, FOE will undertake substantial legislative activity, including lobbying and focusing public attention on critical issues. It will join other organisations in going to court to fight environmental abuse, and wage an all-out war on any interest which ignores the needs of the environment.

FOE's members will form specific task forces supported by teams of environmental experts and citizen's groups. The acronym FOE is appropriate: any friend of the earth must be the foe of whatever or whoever degrades it.

FOE needs support. It has a growing register of Friends who are prepared to fight authorities and industries insensitive to the ecological effects of their activities. If these goals are yours, contact FOE by completing the form on page 177 of this book and sending it to Friends of the Earth, 8 King Street, London, W.C.2. Tel 01-836 0718.

Appendix IV

Bibliography

BARR, JOHN. *The Environmental Handbook.* London: Ballantine Books, 1971. For expanded list of references on population-environmental issues.

BORGSTROM, GEORG. *Too Many: The Biological Limitations of Our Earth.* London: Collier-Macmillan, 1967. An excellent discussion of the limits of food production.

DOMHOFF, G. WILLIAM. *Who Rules America?* London: Prentice-Hall, 1967. A well-documented discussion of the composition of the American ruling class and power elite.

DOMHOFF, G. WILLIAM and HOYT B. BALLARD, eds. *C. Wright Mills and the Power Elite.* Boston: Beacon Press, 1968. A variety of views on who controls the American State.

EHRLICH, PAUL R. *The Population Bomb.* London: Ballantine Books, 1971. A brief, popular description of the population explosion and its effects.

EHRLICH, PAUL R. AND ANNE H. *Population, Resources, Environment: Issues in Human*

Ecology. London: W.H. Freeman, 1970. An attempt at a comprehensive treatment of the current crisis. Extensive annotated bibliographies.

EHRLICH, PAUL R. AND JOHN P. HOLDREN. *Global Ecology: Readings toward a Rational Strategy for Man*. New York: Harcourt, Brace, and Jovanovich, 1971. Contains many of the most important original works in the area.

FELLMETH, ROBERT. *The Interstate Commerce Omission: The Public Interest and the ICC*. New York: Grossman Publishers, 1970. The Ralph Nader study group report on the Interstate Commerce Commission and Transportation.

GALBRAITH, JOHN K. *The New Industrial State*. London: Penguin, 1969. Describes the creation of demand and other aspects of the corporate monster in great detail. Weak on the significance of American overseas investment.

GOFMAN, JOHN W. and TAMPLIN, ARTHUR R. *Population Control Through Nuclear Pollution*. Chicago: Nelson Hall, 1970. A stunning expose of nuclear "safety" as promoted by the Atomic Energy Commission.

HACKER, ANDREW. *The End of the American Era*. New York: Atheneum, 1970. A very gloomy but informative and perhaps realistic view of our future.

HOLLINGS, ERNEST F. *The Case Against Hunger*. New York: Cowles, 1970. How and why the U.S. fails to feed its own people.

KOLKO, GABRIEL. *The Roots of American Foreign Policy*. Boston: Beacon Press, 1969. See especially Chapters 3 and 4 for the role of resource consideration in American foreign policy.

LOCKWOOD, LEE. *Castro's Cuba, Cuba's Fidel*. New York: Vintage Books, 1967. Contains a long, interesting interview in which Castro describes his plans for the semi-development of Cuba.

LUNDBERG, FERDINAND. *The Rich and the Super-Rich: A Study in the Power of Money Today*. London: Nelson, 1969. A detailed description of wealth in America, as contrasted with the American dream.

MEAD, MARGARET. *Culture and Commitment: A Study of the Generation Gap*. Garden City, New York: Doubleday, 1970. A distinguished older scholar considers the counter-culture in anthropological terms.

MYRDAL, GUNNAR. The *Challenge of World Poverty: A World of Anti-Poverty Program in Outline*. New York: Pantheon, 1970. An excellent, though occasionally culture-bound and ecologically naive, treatment of the problems of UDC development.

NADER, RALPH, ed. *Ecotactics*. New York: Pocket Books, 1970. A guide for environmental activists.

NOSSITER, BERNARD D. *Soft State: A Newspaperman's Chronicle of India*. New York and Evanston: Harper & Row, 1970. A very readable popular description of the kinds of problems dealt with by Myrdal.

REICH, CHARLES A. *The Greening of America: The Coming of a New Consciousness and the Rebirth of a Future*. London: Penguin, 1971. A well-written codification of counter-culture ideals; a very hopeful previews of the emergence of new men (Reich calls their attitudes "Consciousness III").

RIENOW, ROBERT AND RIENOW, LEONA TRAIN. *Moment in the Sun*. London: Ballantine Books, 1971. Good overview of environmental deterioration in the United States.

ROSZAK, THEODORE. *The Making of a Counter-Culture: Reflections of the Technocratic Society and its Youthful Opposition*. London: Faber, 1970. One of the first important works on the new men.

THAYER, GEORGE. *The War Business*: *The International Trade in Armaments*. London: Wiedenfeld & Nicholson, 1969. Describes the conventional arms trade in great detail.

YORK, HERBERT. *Race to Oblivion: A Participant's View of The Arms Race*. New York: Simon and Schuster, 1970. A horrifying examination of our military-industrial stupidity from an impeccable source.

Note: at time of printing, many of the above-listed publications are available only in the U.S.

Acknowledgments

The list of colleagues who have contributed ideas to this book and who have devoted time to criticizing our ideas would form a small book in itself. We owe them a deep debt.

Mrs. Patricia A. Singer, Mrs. Christine M. Gilbert and Mrs. Peter Duignan have cheerfully typed repeated drafts, and Jane Lawson Bavelas has helped immensely with editorial chores.

Our deepest debt is to Anne H. Ehrlich who has applied her fine editorial hand to the manuscript and who wrote several sections. She would have been a co-author but declined because, in the tradition of her mother-in-law, she felt the grammar was not up to her standards.

MORE BALLANTINE
CONSERVATION TITLES

THE POPULATION BOMB,
Dr. Paul R. Ehrlich   30p
Overpopulation is now the dominant problem in all our personal, national, and international planning. Dr. Ehrlich clearly describes the dimensions of the crisis in all its aspects, and provides a realistic evaluation of the remaining options.

THE ENVIRONMENTAL HANDBOOK,
edited by John Barr   40p
The 1970's is our last chance for a future that makes ecological sense. The book focuses on some of the major problems of our deteriorating environment, and — more important — suggests action that can be taken immediately in any community, by any individual. Foreword by Kenneth Allsop, and contributors include Sir Frank Fraser Darling, Dr. Paul Ehrlich, Lord Ritchie-Calder, Professor René Dubos and Dr. Kenneth Mellanby.

WILDERNESS AND PLENTY,
Sir Frank Fraser Darling   30p
In his 1969 Reith Lectures, Sir Frank Fraser Darling views the wilderness as a shrinking natural resource, no longer an environment to be conquered by man. He looks toward the future with a plan for conservation and a plan for man's responsibility to nature.

THE CONSUMERS' GUIDE
TO THE PROTECTION
OF THE ENVIRONMENT

JONATHAN HOLLIMAN 40p

It is an ecological fact of life that the goods we buy, and the services we use, effect the environment in which we live. Each penny paid for the product that is harmful or unnecessary, the process that pollutes, the food that does not nourish, prolongs and expands the squandering of our resources and the pollution of the environment on which we ultimately depend.

The Consumers' Guide looks at several major areas of goods and services, and explains simply and clearly the environmental effects of their production, use and disposal.

It is essentially an action guide for the individual. It tells exactly how we can direct our consumer habits so that we can relate our way of life to the ability of the environment to support our real needs.

FRIENDS OF THE EARTH

8, King Street
London WC2E 8HS.

Registration as a Friend ....

Friend and Supporter £3 ....

Friend and Supporter £100 ....

Name: ....

Address: ....

Address: ....

Tel. No. (day) .... (evening) ....

Interests and/or specialised knowledge or training:

Ideas for action:

All cheques should be made payable to Friends of the Earth Ltd. As a company limited by guarantee, all money FOE receives must be devoted to its objects and cannot be distributed.

STYLE OF LIFE BOOKS AVAILABLE FROM BALLANTINE

A SAND COUNTY ALMANAC,
Aldo Leopold 40p

First published in 1949, Aldo Leopold's *A Sand County Almanac* is now an established environmental classic. Beginning with a beautifully written description of the seasonal changes in nature and their effect on the delicate ecological balance, the book gives examples of man's destructive interference with nature and thus expresses the need for areas of wilderness.

PLEASANT VALLEY,
Louis Bromfield 40p

This is the story of one man's lifelong experience with the good earth and how a way of life was restored by going back to organic farming. It is set in the hill country of Ohio, U.S.A.

ROADLESS AREA,
Paul Brooks 40p

Here is the country beyond the maps — the American wilderness, the Alaskan tundra, the game reserves of East Africa and the adventure of the invitation they offer, re-counted with rare beauty and quiet humour.

Take a thoughtful look at the way we live now-adays

your environment
quarterly subscription magazine

discusses the contemporary problems in depth and detail: problems of planning, conservation, use of resources and the quality of life in our increasingly dense, organised societies.

Subscribers represent a broad spectrum of readers with professional and lay interest in environmental issues — in rational technology, good design, socially responsible management and ecological conservation.

If you would like to subscribe and join the list of members in more than 30 countries round the world (including for instance Borneo, Fiji, Malawi, Tasmania and Rumania) please send back to us the coupon below, or write to us for further details.

- - - - - - - - - - - - - - - -

To: your environment, 10 Roderick Road, London NW3 2NL

please enter my subscription for one year at £1.75 for four issues, including postage.*

☐ To begin current issue   ☐ Payment enclosed
☐ To include back issues as available   ☐ Please send invoice

Cheques and postal orders to *'your environment'*, please.
*U.S.A. $5; other overseas $2.00, including post seamail letter rate; airmail rates on application.

NAME: ....

ADDRESS: ....

....

FURTHER CONSERVATION TITLES
AVAILABLE
FROM BALLANTINE BOOKS

CONCORDE: THE CASE AGAINST
   SUPERSONIC TRANSPORT,
   Richard Wiggs   35p

THE FRAIL OCEAN,
   Wesley Marx   40p

SCIENCE AND SURVIVAL,
   Barry Commoner   40p

MOMENT IN THE SUN,
   Robert and Leona Rienow   40p

TEACHING FOR SURVIVAL,
   Mark Terry   40p

THE ALIEN ANIMALS,
   George Laycock   40p

The books advertised here are obtainable from all booksellers and newsagents. If you have any difficulty, please send purchase price plus 5p postage to P.O. Box 11, Falmouth, Cornwall.